Are You Willing?

ARE YOU WILLING?

Sharing The Greatest Treasure
Stories About Loving All People with
Grace, Mercy and Truth

DEBORAH AND RICHARD SAINT
SOPHIA ASAH AND FRIENDS

XULON PRESS

Xulon Press
2301 Lucien Way #415
Maitland, FL 32751
407.339.4217
www.xulonpress.com

Edited by Karen Porter, Bold Vision Books

Printed in the United States of America.

ISBN-13:978-1-5456-7298-3

"I believe in Christianity as I believe that the sun has risen: not only because I see it, but because by it I see everything else." *~C.S. Lewis*

"There is enough power in the cross to solve the world's problems, but we Christians have not used it." *~Frank Buchman*

Table of Contents

Foreword

It is an interesting adventure and call to be a shepherd, a Pastor, to all kinds of people. Sometimes a couple will enter a Pastor's circle of influence and they will be very raw, real and needy or poor in spirit. The honesty to share grief, desperate emotions, a variety of ongoing difficulties and traumas of life takes courage and trust. Thankfully, when participants are willing to trust and follow God's leading, not perfectly but authentically and repentantly when failures surface, The Lord will be in our midst in His special ways. This is the case with Richard and Deborah.

In the process of ministering to them and praying for and with them, and being in God's Word together, the influence of the Holy Spirit and the mercy and grace of God became more evident and impactful to my wife and me. The goal of experiencing the Presence of God and the reality of the Risen Christ and His resurrection anointing being believed in and being lived out in daily faith is one in which we share. In this endeavor The Gospel is experienced at a new level and prayerfully with ignited faith.

Their story is a hard one. It is more common than most are willing to admit. They admit their story to bring forth God's story of salvation, redemption and restoration. There are many out there who will relate to them in one or more ways.

Restoration is such a big part of the transformation God desires to bring forth in the lives of His children. My wife and I have witnessed our Lord bringing forth His restoration in this couple—in their lives and health. We have watched the promises of God's forgiveness, acceptance and love take greater root in their lives as they have grown to love, forgive and accept themselves, each other and others more. Their desire is to live out the Gospel and show the resurrection power of God in their very lives. They have shared their goal of living true to Revelation 12:11 by applying the finished works of Christ to their lives and future by giving testimony to what God has and is still doing by His grace!

In her previous book, "The Elephant Gospel, Unshackled to Live the Secret of Hope", Deborah Ann Saint opens her life and heart for anyone to see and hear what our mutual enemy, Satan, the devil, does not want anyone to hear....that no matter what we have done or what others have done to us, Jesus Christ has exposed and triumphed over our sin, our secret shame and fear and has offered unconditional hope and help through His cross and resurrection! Deb's life story is shared in this book but so is her testimony of what Christ has done and most importantly, what Christ has offered to all of us....it really is so much more than what we may now realize!

The Word of God through His Gospel is abundant throughout the pages of this book. I personally appreciate the way the truths of the Gospel are clearly applied to real life disappointments and soul woundings. Just like a physician treating a patient with a health issue in their area of specialty, the Holy Spirit speaks specifically and powerfully to bring healing and deliverance. If you want to receive hope and healing, please read this book and find a quiet place to meditate on it's contents. You may find yourself weeping with tears of hope and joy! Yes, it's that good!

Pastor Dan Groff,
Sarasota-Bradenton, Florida

Introduction

"Some who pick up this book may make no claim to know God. Others may make the claim but be victims of the self-delusion that John observes. (1 John 2:4-6) Yet others may know Him, and obey Him, but wonder sometimes at the value of this knowledge and this obedience. I think that this book will have something to say to all three. If those in the first category want to know God, they may perhaps learn how. Those in the second group may find that they are missing a great deal by not backing their claims with action. And those in the third category may be encouraged to pursue their course."

-Elisabeth Elliott, *Shadow of the Almighty*

When I read Elizabeth Elliot's preface to her amazing book *Shadow of the Almighty,* I realized that there will also likely be three groups who will read this book: those who make no claim to know Him yet; those who claim to know Him but maybe don't; and those who know and obey Him. If you are like me, you have probably lived part of your life in each of these groups. And, like me, you know people who fall into each group.

With this understanding, my husband and some friends have joined me in telling some of our stories on these pages. Together, we seek to yield ourselves to the Lord and open our hearts to give to the reader what we have received. We want to grow and to be prepared to help others grow, especially in wisdom, character, stature, unity, and favor. (See Ephesians 4:13, 2 Peter 1:2,8) We believe *the strength of grace* is a compelling force in all our stories and lives, and through our stories, we hope to exalt Christ as Paul did and motivate our readers to live out in greater measure the fullness of God's love and truth: the Gospel.

We share in our stories the amazing ways God has forgiven and blessed us. Through the best of times and the worst of times, good choices and poor choices—some that might make you uncomfortable—we authors have come to know the Lord and His love. In writing together, we are choosing to walk out our faith in new and bold ways because Jesus gave all for us.

The following true, concise (and hopefully effectual) accounts represent some of the most important or pivotal moments in our lives. Because, in these events, it seems God has intervened in powerful ways to demonstrate and make a show of the greatness of His redemption and the enormity of His Grace and Mercy. His transformations, restorations and reconciliations are miracles to behold. We believe, through these stories, the reality, truth and hope of the Gospel will be evident as it is applied in practical and encouraging ways that often intersect with the cultural hot topics of our day.

We hope the reader will gain greater perspective, insight and willingness to live out, in a fuller measure, Gospel truths and love in these tough life situations that are so prevalent today. We also hope to equip readers to be increasingly cognizant of where people are coming from, in their hurts and their needs and differences. In this way, the reader may more effectively navigate and live out grace and truth with great love.

Our prayer is that through the power of the cross, the resurrection, and our testimonials, God's Word and His Spirit will be at work in us all as we read and learn and grow together to impact our world for Christ and His Kingdom.

Our dream is for all of us to align ourselves as Christ's Body through the unity of the Holy Spirit—to be those who know Him and obey Him— out of sheer love, gratitude and trust for His amazing goodness and grace. We want to walk in the power of His resurrection by His Holy Spirit and not be ashamed of the Gospel for it is the power of God that brings salvation to those who believe! (Romans 1:16) Would it not be wonderful if our generation would be the answer and fulfillment to Jesus' prayer in John 17? (The Chapter of John 17 is printed at end of this book.)

~Deborah, Richard, Sophia and our friends

Chapter One

Will You Join Us?
Richard

Anyone who does not love does not know God, because God is love. (1 John 4:8 ESV)

"Come, follow Me," Jesus said, "and I will make you fishers of men."
(Matthew 4:19-20 Berean Study Bible)

Have you ever had a dream that so touched your heart that you felt truly changed by it? I recently had such a dream. Whether this dream was from the Lord (which I believe it was) or was only a picture of what I had been considering while I was awake, I do not know for sure. However, I am thankful for the dream, and I pray that God will give my wife and me the chance to show our hearts this way.

In the dream, I was back at my old high school. I am not sure whether I was a teacher at the high school or whether I was there for some other reason.

One of my initial interactions, while at the school, was with one of the students. This student was a thin young man, disheveled and dirty. It was clear that he was not part of the *in crowd* at the high school. He seemed bitter about everything and disliked everything that was around him. I tried to speak to him, but he gave me a scowl and moved away.

As he moved away, it became clear that he was ill. He started coughing loudly. All the other students seemed to vanish into the many classrooms, and the young man and I were left alone in the hallway. He began moving toward the restroom. As he got closer to the restroom, he began to vomit. He was seriously sick. He staggered toward the bathroom and entered through the swinging door. I saw the mess in the hallway but I could also hear that he was continuing to vomit in the bathroom. For some reason, I felt that I had the responsibility to try to help this young man and to clean up the mess he was causing.

I entered the bathroom to check on the young man. Not only was he still vomiting, he was taking the vomit and wiping it on the walls, sink, and mirrors. He seemed to take an evil pleasure in what he was doing—like this was his revenge. I felt disgust, yet at the same time, there was no doubt in my mind that I had to clean everything.

The young man finally stopped vomiting and sat down in the corner of the restroom. I began the process of cleaning up his mess. I remember wondering what sort of illness or disease that I was exposing myself to, by way of the cleanup. But in my dream, I did not have a choice. I completed the cleanup process.

At the end of the cleanup, the principal of the high school came into the restroom. Somehow, he knew what had happened, and he also seemed to feel that it was my responsibility to cleanup as well. He checked the restroom and found all to be clean and in order. The principal then left. The young man also decided to leave the restroom. I followed him to see what else he would do.

He went outside the school and walked toward a car. There were three other young men in the car. The front passenger seat was empty so the sick young man got into the car and sat in that seat.

All four young men looked at me with mocking sneers. They asked me why I was looking at them. I stood still. The sick young man advised me that they were all gay and he looked at me to see how I would respond. The driver of the car started to accuse me of being "like all the others" and that I had no right to condemn them. I remember feeling so sad. I could feel their pain as they assumed that I would condemn them for their lifestyle.

I guess my sadness was reflected on my face. The driver said, "Look at him. It almost looks like he cares. I know better, though. No one cares."

Then he seemed to soften, "No one has ever spoken to us with any help or guidance." He continued, "We only talk to each other and no girls will ever speak to us."

I said, "I know people who will speak with you. I know people who care about you and will try to help you."

The sick young man said, "Who?"

Before I could answer, I woke up. Just as I was opening my mouth to respond to the sick young man, I left the dream. My heart and my emotions, however, were still caught up in the strong feelings that I had felt in standing near those young men. I could still feel their lostness and desperation for direction and acceptance.

As I lay in the bed, I heard the sick young man's question. "Who?"

I want to give them names of those **who *are willing* to help**. I want to give them names of people **who *are willing* to share the gospel message** so that these young men, or anyone who does not know the gospel message, can feel the hope and strength that only comes from a saving relationship with Jesus Christ. Could I give them your name? Could I assure these young men that you **would be willing** to meet with them to share the truth of the gospel and provide them with a pathway to purpose and meaning in their lives? I know my wife and I are willing to share. **Will you join us?**

Prayer

Heavenly Father, Jesus said, "Go into all the world and preach the gospel to all creation (Mark 16:15a). Help us do as You commissioned us Lord. Help us realize Your Word and warnings are true and there is much at stake. Help us love as Christ loved us and be willing to show His love and acceptance to those You put in our paths and to all people. We pray that we will share Christ and our faith may become effective for the full knowledge of every good thing that is in us for the sake of Christ (Philemon 1:6). Thank You LORD that the Spirit God gave us, gives us power, love and self-discipline and does not make us timid or afraid. Cause us not to be ashamed of the testimony about our Lord or of those radically born-anew like Paul (2 Timothy 1:7-8). Holy Spirit teach us what we should say at the time we should say it (Luke 12:12). In our weakness when we do not know what we ought to pray for, Holy Spirit, thank You that You intercede for us (Romans 8:26). LORD, help us to be prayerful, depend on You, and have confidence in Your leading. We pray we would hear Your direction and obey You. May we experience You and ***proclaim*** *what we have seen and heard of* ***Jesus so that many*** **will join us in fellowship with the Father and with his Son Jesus Christ.** Help us **be willing to join** with other believers **to share Christ and even to suffer for the gospel, by the power of God** (1 John 1:3). In Jesus' Name, Amen.

Chapter Two

The Wide-Open Door
Deborah

"For I delivered to you as of first importance what I also received: that Christ died for our sins in accordance with the Scriptures, that he was buried, that he was raised on the third day in accordance with the Scriptures" (1 Corinthians 15:3-5 NKJV)

"God has not been trying an experiment on my faith or love in order to find out their quality. He knew it already. It was I who didn't. In this trial...He always knew that my temple was a house of cards. His only way of making me realize the fact was to knock it down." ~ CS Lewis

This CS Lewis quote touched a nerve in me and stirred my heart as I wondered about my own life. What is the quality of my faith and love? Is my temple a house of cards? Will those with whom I share my faith see a "house of cards" in me? How can I rebuild on a firmer foundation? With a firmer foundation, how can I successfully share the Good News with people? I hope these questions are ideas you and I will explore for answers together through this book.

The Wide-Open Door

The door near me was wide open. It seemed strange it would be left that way. The medical staff had escorted the very-sick looking patient past me and into the exam room. This man inside sounded as if he could use some privacy. He was so near and yet so far away—only eight to ten feet from where I rested on a makeshift bed in the narrow hallway while receiving an IV—but the formal separation of the exam room was a barrier not to be breeched.

His cough sounded awful, the worst I probably have ever heard. Suffering and agony echoed loud in those cavernous sounds like a last-days kind of cough. The mood of the clinic environment seemed to shadow his coughing crisis.

Was he dying? My tears and my raw emotions surprised me in their force, sudden and keenly felt. From somewhere deep, memories were tapped and unexpected pain afflicted me. I felt I was given compassion for and an awareness of this man's plight in a way that seemed unusual, maybe supernatural?

Did this man know the Lord? Should I try to find a way to talk to him? And then more personal questions rushed in. *Would I be willing to share Christ and expose myself to his illness? Would I be willing to suffer his illness in order for him to be saved? Would I be willing to risk getting what he had and potentially die, even if he is still not saved?*

I thought about how Jesus had died for me while I was still a sinner and how He offers the same gift to all, yet many will reject His offer. He knew He would die for many that would reject Him. I realized anew the enormity of Jesus' love and sacrifice for me, for this man, for all of us. The man's desperate-seeming state brought Jesus' love into greater focus and to fuller life for me.

I desired to bring him Christ's love, forgiveness, and living hope which I received and knew. It is such a great gift and so available and there is so much at stake to miss or reject it. I began a repeat dialogue within myself.

"What cost would I be ***willing*** *to pay to give out the gospel to* ***anyone,*** *whether straight, gay, homeless, outcast, misfit, a Pharisee, an atheist, one good in their own eyes, someone medically contagious, someone dangerous… anyone?"*

"Would I really give my life?"

"What is the value of a soul?" "Valuable enough that Jesus gave His life."

"Will I trust God to lead me and to know when to go?"

"I do want to trust God, but I admit I'm hesitant and feel powerless and uncertain how to proceed."

"Do I really believe what I believe?"

"Yes, I do believe, but if I speak what I believe, would the man reject me as a religious fanatic or would he sense God's love, compassion, care and concern and the hope offered?" Would I portray "a house of cards"?

The experience opened my eyes wide. My heart longed to be wide open and infuse hope and life into this man.

His coughing reminded me of patients I had cared for as a nurse. Worse, it reminded me of my parents who both died of respiratory illnesses.[1] It was all too fresh and awful. In addition, during most of my childhood, I shared a room with my younger sister who had severe asthma. Her breathing crises were unforgettably traumatic. More than once I raced from my bed at night to get my mother so she could help my sister's desperate state, gasping for life. It was hard to watch my sister struggle for every breath. It seemed terrifying to have to gasp for air. She was in ICU for breathing issues twice. This man's struggle was terrifying as well.

All these memories of my parents and sister flooded back. Tears streamed down my face. The fact that I was identifying this unknown man with family members and long-ago memories felt both endearing and frightening. I prayed for him yet my prayers seemed small and not impactful.

I never talked to the man. When my therapy ended, he was undergoing some kind of treatment, and there was no access readily available to me. I returned home. I realized the conflict raging in me. I wondered how I could have such a strong emotional experience and yet not follow up with actions. This inaction disturbed me and again caused me to think of "a house of cards". I was affected and challenged, and a desire grew in me to do more to live truer to the gospel. I began to realize "the cards" needed to be removed from my life and I needed to build on Christ as my firm foundation. There was much work to do for me to overcome the old structure and rebuild my life.Without knowing it then, this experience and others would hit even closer than I ever imagined and in a revelatory personal way that surprised and challenged me.

"Revival occurs when those who think they already know the gospel discover they do not really or fully know it. This leads to repentance and change." - Tim Keller[2]

"But woe to you, scribes and Pharisees, hypocrites! For you shut the kingdom of heaven in people's faces. For you neither enter yourselves nor allow those who would enter to go in" (Matthew 23:13 ESV).

This verse comes to my mind often and as I consider it, I wonder if I am *anything like these scribes and Pharisees?* I know I have been a hypocrite too many times to count. I would not want Jesus to pronounce a *woe* over me, or anyone, so I have self-examined and repented and asked the Lord how to enter the door of the kingdom of heaven more fully. (I know I am born-again but I sometimes find myself acting like a Pharisee.) I want to change, and I want to lead others to the door—not block them from entering. Jesus said, I am the door: by me if any man enter in, he shall be saved, and shall go in and out, and find pasture (John 10:9). However, my dilemma is how to lead others to enter in real life and to encourage others likewise.

In contemplating this, I realized that having belief and confidence in "who is the door" is important. Jesus is an advocate with the Father—the Righteous One. (1 John 2:1) Jesus is the only way to the Father (John 14:6; John 6:44, John 6:65). God is a Just and Righteous Judge, The Sovereign Lord, my refuge, One who is good to be near, my God (Psalm 73:28). He wants me to tell of his works and bring others to Christ, the door. He is welcoming, merciful and delights to forgive (Exodus 34:6-7; Psalm 89:14; Psalm 145:8-9)

He wants me/us to intercede in prayer for others with faith, respect, holy fear of Him and with a bold passion for The Kingdom of God and the saving of souls, much like Abraham did in Genesis 18.[3]

Prayer

Lord, help those who know You to be gracious, led by Your Spirit, and not hindered or stuck in Pharisee-like hypocrisy and unbelief that blocks the door, Christ, the way to the Kingdom of God. Help us repent of unbelief, self-righteousness, un-love or any other attitude/sin that turns people away from Christ. LORD, help us to be an intercessor like Abraham as we pray, trusting in Your faithful goodness and promises to save those who will believe. May we have faith in You, Lord, as the Judge of all the Earth. May we trust Jesus, the Righteous One and the Holy Spirit as our Advocate with the Father, (1 John 2:1; John 14:16, 26; 15:26; 16:7). We ask for Your help, counsel, and advice. May we live depending on You.

Please continue to delight in mercy on us when we fail (Micah 7:18). Lord, please make our heart's desire and prayers to You be for Israel and the lost, that they might be saved. (Romans 10:1) Please Lord, help us have hearts to offer supplications, prayers, intercessions, and the giving of thanks for all men. (1 Timothy 2:1-6). Thank you that the Son of man came to seek and to save that which was lost. (Luke 19:10) Thank you Lord for telling us that Your desire is to have all men to be saved, and to come unto the knowledge of the truth (1 Timothy 2:4). Father, please draw them to You so they might come to Your Son and be raised up at the last day. (John 6:44) Please move again LORD by your Spirit in your people. May we take steps to live true to Christ in boasting on our weaknesses: sharing our testimony of Your grace, as You lead. Help us show how You care and how You give Your appropriate touch with love and compassion. May we not be ashamed of Your Gospel as it is the power of God to salvation for any who will believe. Help us ***be willing*** **to share effectively and with audacious confidence in Your power to save to the uttermost.** (Romans 1:16; 2 Peter 3:9; Hebrews 7:25) In Jesus' Name, Amen.

Chapter Three

Wide-Open Heart
Deborah

"…give me your heart, and let your eyes observe my ways" (Proverbs 23:26 ESV).

"We have spoken freely to you, Corinthians; ***our heart is wide open.*** *You are not restricted by us, but you are restricted in your own affections. In return* ***widen your hearts*** *also"*

(2 Corinthians 6:11-13 ESV Emphasis Mine)

These verses call us to give our hearts to God and to *widen our hearts to others.* As I reflect on the events in that clinic, I realize I did not actively seek an opportunity to speak to this coughing man. My heart was not wide open to him. In truth, I was partly relieved and partly sad that I did not speak to him. In my deepest heart, I wondered what I would say to him. (I guess, I did not believe I could make a difference. That showed me I was trusting in "my house of cards"-that his response was somehow my responsibility and not God's.) It seemed a relief that I was not given an opportunity. Clearly I was in conflict.

I asked questions of myself that you might want to ask of yourself as well: *"How wide open is my heart?" God wants us to enlarge our hearts? How do you and I accomplish it?*

For me, widening my heart begins with an admission of my need for change. I must repent and then turn to Christ for more faith to believe that He brings results. I simply need to **be willing to share** and be persistent to follow through and depend on The Lord. I pray for a wider opened heart, moved to action in caring and to sharing Christ.

The truth of how much God loves me despite my failures, and how He has forgiven me and given me mercy and grace, compels me to want to share my faith with others. However, I feel inadequate about how to share Jesus and the gospel to people. I have lived religiously so long "in my house of cards" that I need revival in my life and a new dependence on the Holy Spirit.

****

When I was writing my first book *The Elephant Gospel, a* pastor encouraged me to engage the LGBTQ community with the truth of the gospel. Joining a ministry for Christians with an LGBTQ history and hearing their stories, made clear to me my shortcomings and my inability in myself to make any difference at all, unless the Holy Spirit was at work in me. I found my work-based faith hindered God's Spirit. Due to "my works and pride" I confess that I have treated others as less than or inferior. Sadly, I was self-righteous, fearful and judgmental. (This is similar to the way church people have sometimes treated me in the past.) By interacting with others with similar histories as mine, I faced my worst self: my worst sins. I had to identify with those whose life experiences were similar to mine. I had to learn how to live the gospel by extending grace to myself and to them. I had to grow through the Holy Spirit in a way I had not known before.

The adage, "Children learn what they live" is true in my life. I have been indoctrinated into "works-based" Christianity and I have focused on what I am doing, rather than focusing completely on the Lord. My works were my "house of cards". To die to self and live for Christ is not just another expression or Bible verse, it is an act of God, (and the truth of God) at work in born-again believers.

When I was treated by other Christians with self-righteous, prideful, religious, unloving, and unaccepting attitudes, I was never drawn to Christ. I know these attitudes will not help others either. It is no wonder so many want nothing to do with Jesus when they are confronted with those with these attitudes and approaches. God's people often do not represent Him well. (Sadly, myself included.) I pray to give my heart more fully to the Lord to be open-hearted and allow His Holy Spirit to change me and for Him to do what only He can by His Spirit.

In America, many people know about Jesus but are turned off with "Christians" who show little, if any, evidence of the love and life of Christ. It seems familiarity with these type Christians has bred contempt for Christ. People seem to know the words of John 3:16 but not the reality of this truth. **Unless those who don't know the Lord *see transformation in us who do know Him, and unless they feel love from us,* they will never want to know the Truth.** It is as if we are preaching a different gospel instead of the Truth. We want to represent Christ well by allowing Him to be in control. Let us ask of our Heavenly Father for more of His Holy Spirit. (Luke 11:13, Acts 8:14-17)

We do not want it said of us, what Paul said of the Galatians:

"I marvel that ye are so soon removed from him that called you into the grace of Christ unto ***another gospel****: which is not another; but there be some that trouble you, and would pervert the gospel of Christ. But though we, or an angel from heaven, preach any other gospel unto you than that which we have preached unto you, let him be accursed. As I said before, so say I now again, if any man preach any other gospel unto you than that ye have received, let him be accursed" (Galatians 1:6-9 KJV Emphasis Mine).*

"For if someone comes and proclaims ***another Jesus*** *than the one we proclaimed, or if you receive* ***a different spirit*** *from the one you received, or if you accept* ***a different gospel*** *from the one you accepted, you put up with it readily enough" (2 Corinthians 11:4 ESV Emphasis Mine)*

But instead we want to live the great commission with these truths at work in our lives and in our messages:

"Now I would remind you, brothers, ***of the gospel I preached to you, which you received, in which you stand, and by which you are being saved,*** *if you hold fast to the word I preached to you—unless you believed in vain. For I delivered to you* ***as of first importance what I also received: that Christ died for our sins in accordance with the Scriptures, that he was buried, that he was raised on the third day in accordance with the Scriptures"*** *(1 Corinthians 15:1-4 ESV Emphasis Mine)*

Most people in America have someone in their family, friends or sphere of influence who have completely different lifestyles and world-views. How we were raised, our life experiences and what we thus believe affects how we interact and relate to others. The biggest challenge in my life and in this book is: ***Are we willing*** **to relate and live the gospel, the truth, to those who are different from us, in their lifestyles and beliefs?**

How do we, as believers in Christ, show God's love and live true to His Word in the midst of church and cultural divisions due to differing beliefs and world views?

Since opening up my story to first one person, then another trusted person, then a few people, then a small group, then larger groups and now open to the public by the book *The Elephant Gospel,* I have learned that the more I tell my story, the freer I become. I am more accepting of the truth of who I have been and more aware of the forgiveness, grace and mercy I have received from the Lord. Sadly, I have also learned that telling my real story has brought judgments, rejection, disappointments, risks, bad advice, abuses—and a feeling that

the gospel is on trial in all of us. As Christians, we are called to live Christ and share Christ in the truest sense of the gospel.

Have you ever seen the movie *Overboard* with Goldie Hawn and Kurt Russell? I love this movie! To me, the best thing about the movie is that *after* horrible trauma to include amnesia, betrayal, abuse, and a near death experience, Joanna, the main character, is no longer the same woman she once was. She has come to experience love and compassion and has broken out of her old existence into an experience of purpose, love, and hope like she has never known.

In the movie, Joanna sees the truth of who she used to be and how she had been living by the standards she was taught to live. Her perspectives had been so narrow and limited. She came to see how much richer and more fulfilling life can be when love and purpose are involved.

"A God kind of transformation" has happened to me through sufferings, and different situations that caused me to wake up and be **willing** to see the futility of self-works-based—futile-type living. I then began to live the true gospel to myself and others. I have in a sense, jumped off the ship of works-based religion and its judgments. I have embraced the truth of who I used to be and how what I had been taught was not all there is to know. Life is much richer and more fulfilling when the Spirit of God is at work and love, truth and gospel purpose are involved.

Understanding myself and gaining peace with my past are being achieved through the Gospel. I know where I have been, that God's plans are good, and where I am going (Jeremiah 29:11; John 14;1-3). **I have experienced that the gospel is precious, that Jesus is real, and life can be good.** I believe the Lord reveals Himself and His Gospel to us more and more as we walk with Him and He teaches us His Truth. He promises to guide us into all Truth. Jesus is the good Life.

"When the Spirit of truth comes, he will guide you into all the truth, for he will not speak on his own authority, but whatever he hears he will speak, and he will declare to you the things that are to come" (John 16:13 ESV).

"Teach me your way, Lord, that I may rely on your faithfulness; give me an undivided heart, that I may fear your name" (Psalm 86:11 NIV).

"...Jesus said, 'If you hold to my teaching, you are really my disciples. Then you will know the truth, and the truth will set you free'" (John 8:31-32 NIV).

Prayer

LORD, help us know Your heart of love for us. Please help us give You our hearts to open them wide. We love because You first loved us (1 John 4:19). Help Your love show in our lives. Help us understand to a greater measure the wonder of Your love at the Cross and our receiving Your gift and sacrifice for us! Help us recognize to a greater revelation the result of receiving You is "being born from above": having the Holy Spirit indwell us! Please help us live in and from this born from above state in communion/relationship with You, Lord Jesus and Your Father. Please make the presence of the Holy Spirit real to us and apparent in us. We ask for more of the Holy Spirit to manifest in and through us. (Luke 11:13) Cause our salvation experience and its transformation to be evident in us. Teach us Your way, Lord, that we may rely on Your faithfulness; give me/us an undivided heart, that I/we may fear Your name and hold to Your teachings. Let our eyes observe Your ways, to know Your truth and be free. ***Let us not be restricted in our own affections. Cause us to be willing for our affections to be for You and Your kingdom.*** Help us believe Your plans for us are good and help us consider Heaven now and in our future. Help us speak freely to others as Paul did to the Corinthians with ***our hearts wide open.*** May we decrease so You will increase in us, Lord (John 3:30). **May we be willing to truly show Your heart to the world. May a *widening of our hearts to others demonstrate Your heart of Love to them, In Jesus' Name, Amen.***

Chapter Four

The Four Firehouse Chronicles
Deborah

"I pray that the eyes of your heart may be enlightened, so that you will know what is the hope of His calling, what are the riches of the glory of His inheritance in the saints"

(Ephesians 1:18 NASB).

"For Paul, being ***"filled with the Spirit" is to have the gospel driven into the very center of your being*** *so that rather than just abstract doctrines,* ***it becomes a living reality that affects your whole life.*** *That is what it means to be filled with the Spirit. The Bible is a book given to us to authoritatively guide us, regardless of what century we live in, regardless of what culture we live in." - Tim Keller*

Firehouse Chronicles, #1, #2, #3, and #4 are true experiences that happened to me over the course of several years and are told in chronological order. I share these experiences to show how God is present and active in our lives to accomplish things we could not achieve on our own. As we listen for the Lord's direction and obey as we believe He is leading us, He accomplishes His will in and through us. It is exciting and marvelous (and clear in God's Word) how a relationship with Christ brings His leading and His good works in our lives (Ephesians 2:10). As we grow in Him, He prepares us through our past experiences and promises us healing, redemption, restoration and so much more. Our call and inheritance become more exciting as He reveals His work in a visible way. In these events, I believe, this is true.

In the Four Firehouse Chronicles, it is also my hope to show the scarlet thread of redemption connecting my past with my present. These connections may surprise the reader as they did me. Discussing how the events of my past and present tie together in these chronicles is meant to "show off the gospel" and demonstrate an understanding that our world needs the gospel. In other words, in these four stories, **the experiences I once feared would destroy me, were connected, sewn, and pieced together by the Holy Spirit to strengthen and prepare me to live true to the Gospel.**

"Come now, let us reason together, says the LORD: though your sins are like scarlet, they shall be as white as snow; though they are red like crimson, they shall become like wool (Isaiah 1:18 ESV).

Like Rahab, in Joshua 2, I have trusted in the scarlet cord that saves. "The scarlet thread", pointing to and symbolic of the blood of Christ and the need for man's reconciliation with God, runs throughout the Bible. On this side of the cross, Jesus Christ's sacrifice, His shed blood for the forgiveness of sins, and redemption of mankind, have been made known and available to any who will believe.

Perhaps as you read these Firehouse Chronicles, you will see similarities in your life which point the way to God's calling for you? Let's pray together for the Lord to do so and even more than we ask or imagine. (See Ephesians 1:15-19 and 3:20)

Have you ever considered what the purpose of God is for you and for your generation? As we go on this adventure with God, may we discover His answer for us individually and yearn and progress to serve the purpose of God for our generation.

"For David, after ***he had served the purpose of God in his own generation,*** *fell asleep and was laid with his fathers…." (Acts 13:36 ESV Emphasis Mine).*

I consider the Firehouse Chronicles as great gifts from God to me and I hope that they will be to you. I am both humbled and grateful to have experienced these events. I pray these Firehouse Chronicles will challenge you to **pray the prayers of Paul and ask the LORD to answer Paul's prayers in your life.** (For your convenience, The Lord's Prayer, Jesus' High Priestly Prayer in John 17, followed by Paul's prayers, are written out at the end of this book.)

Sharing the Firehouse Chronicles will include some of my past which may be uncomfortable. Yet, through Christ, my past brings me to a place of grace and knowing my calling. The Firehouse Chronicles touch on sensitive, vital, but yet common issues of our time. These are not always easy topics. However, I hope to show that discussing them is profitable when we apply the solution of God's amazing grace. God seemed to orchestrate these moments for a greater purpose than I originally knew.

Prayer

Heavenly Father, as I share these events in the next chapters, please use them to show how incredibly forgiving, gracious, loving, personal, merciful, exciting and redemptive You are. For those who do not know You, draw them to Jesus so they might repent and know His love and forgiveness. Help us more fully understand the power of Christ's cross and resurrection. Teach us how to more closely walk with Jesus by His Holy Spirit and Word. Help us see our past in the light of God's redemption and to use that redeemed past in our individual callings. Help us seek intimacy with You and sense Your guidance to walk in the good works you prepared for us (Ephesians 2:10). Please bring greater revelation and persuasion to Your people regarding the magnitude of their salvation and Your desire that they share their faith with others. Help us better believe Your love for us and then share Your love with others. Help us be thankful for and understanding of Christ's sacrifice on the Cross for the forgiveness of our sins. Help us be happy in Jesus, passionate, authentic, gracious, caring and desirous that others experience Your Presence and Great Salvation. Please, God, show up in our lives and help us delight to do Your Will each day. Help us pray Jesus' prayers and Paul's prayers and may these yield fruit—even today, in our lives. Specifically, we ask You to start by opening the eyes of our hearts to be enlightened, so that we will know what is the hope of Your calling, what are the riches of the glory of Your inheritance in the saints" (Ephesians 1:18). Now unto You we pray as You are able to do exceeding abundantly above all that we ask or think, according to the power that works in us (Ephesians 3:20). Help us **be willing to know Christ's truth, purposes, and gospel power for us individually to fulfill the purpose of our generation and to uphold the foundations of our faith in truth, grace and love.** In Jesus' Name, Amen

Chapter Five

Firehouse Chronicle #1
Deborah

Blessed is the one whose transgression is forgiven, whose sin is covered. Blessed is the man against whom the Lord counts no iniquity, and in whose spirit, there is no deceit. I acknowledged my sin to you, and I did not cover my iniquity; I said, 'I will confess my transgressions to the Lord,' and you forgave the iniquity of my sin. Selah I will instruct you and teach you in the way you should go; I will counsel you with my eye upon you"

(Psalm 32:1-2,5,8 ESV).

"I tell you, her sins—and they are many—have been forgiven, so she has shown me much love. But a person who is forgiven little shows only little love" (Luke 7:47 NLT).

Firehouse Chronicle #1

I drove to Atlanta today to meet my husband. The plan was that he would meet me at a hotel after his plane arrived. He had asked me to pick up take-out for our dinner together. As the time approached, I prayed about where to stop. I took an exit for a Chick-fil-A, but I could not find it. I came across a Firehouse restaurant instead. It seemed like the right place because Firehouse is also a favorite of ours.

I had enjoyed my road trip to Atlanta because I listened to a recording of a teaching on Job. I was happy, relaxed, and full of the Lord's Word, and promises. It seemed the Lord had specifically prepared me for what was to come in a way I had not expected. I entered the restaurant, ordered our sandwiches, and got our drinks at the unique drink dispenser for which Firehouse is known. As I put the lids on our drinks, I saw a wad of money on the floor. I picked it up and counted four one-hundred dollar bills. I have rarely seen a one-hundred-dollar bill. Now, I had four one-hundred dollar bills in my hand. What a surprise!

With the four hundred dollars hidden in my hand, I went to the cashier and said that I had found some money. I said that if anyone had lost some money and they could tell me the exact amount, I would give it back.

The man making the sandwiches said, "Is it four one-hundred dollar bills? Because I just gave that amount to my girlfriend. She was standing right over there." He pointed to the exact spot where I found the money. I nodded. He said, "She must have dropped it. I can't believe she would drop it right after I gave it to her." He seemed annoyed and angry.

As I handed him the money, I said, "If I weren't a good person you'd be out $400." As soon as the words came out of my mouth, I knew better, I felt the Holy Spirit was teaching me. *Am I back to that thinking again?* I knew what that thought meant. The "good person, works-based faith" which had a long hindering history with me was rearing its ugly head again. I knew in my heart that I am fully forgiven and that it is through His Spirit alone that I am able to do His good works that produce eternal fruit.

The gentle wisdom of the Holy Spirit was there to remind me of the difference. Yes, I had done a good deed, but not because I was "a good person." I knew myself and my past. Those two words, *good person,* have tripped me up for so long. Trying to be good through my good works had been my religion, but I knew it was not true Christianity. The moment I stated that I was good I realized I was not saying it to honor God but to honor myself.

Experiencing the goodness of God through the work of Christ has brought such a gift and blessing from the deposit of Christ's righteousness by the indwelling of the Holy Spirit. Only through the working of the Holy Spirit do good works, that bear God's fruit, come forth. (Matthew 5:16, 1 Corinthians 10:31) This understanding is so different from believing I am good on my own.

I thought about the difference between these opposing beliefs and wondered how to correct my statement to the people who had initially heard me. I got the courage to go back up to the counter and said as loud as I could, "It's not because I am a good person but because I am a Christian."

I felt like an idiot. Two of the bystanders were gone but others heard. I wasn't exactly sure why it was so important to make this declaration, but it felt right. My saying this, did open the door for me to converse with the other sandwich maker who declared his understanding as a believer in Christ. Plus, I would later gain a greater understanding of why all of this really was important. At that moment, though, I was sad that I hadn't initially honored God for He surely has been good to me.

The sandwich maker, (the boyfriend) had gone out to the parking lot. I could see him and a young lady through the window. They looked like they were in a heated fight. Their anger seemed excessive. I didn't know why. With my order in hand, I headed for my car. Their voices quieted down as I approached. I asked if I could talk with them. Although I was unsure of what was happening between them, I felt sure that the Lord had brought me there. I told them that I hadn't planned to come to Firehouse Subs, "My being here at that exact moment was not an accident" They stared at me. Then I asked, "Why are you both so angry? You have the money back?" There was an awkward pause and some mumbling about a hole in the girlfriend's pocket. I silently questioned whether the anger was due to the girlfriend's carelessness with the money. I remembered how my husband had lost his wallet and how it had affected us both and had put me in danger at the time. I briefly acknowledged an understanding of the anger and told them of our experience and how it affected me. Then I found myself sharing with them about how my husband and I had been married 33 years and had been through ups and downs. Even though I had said I was a good person, I was not always good. Then I blurted out how I had been forced to have an abortion in our first year of marriage and that even though I had had an abortion, God has forgiven me. I sensed a great tension. There was a strange, pressure-filled pause. That is when I impulsively blurted out words that surprised me, "I hope that the money wasn't for an abortion!"

They looked eye-to-eye at each other. I sensed a challenge and a threat in the exchange and an intensity in this awkward pause.

Once my words were out I could not take them back. I felt so uncomfortable to have said that, and I feared I was way out of line. I had not planned on saying that nor had I desired to corner them or intrude in their business this way. I had impulsively blurted out that statement. *It was as if the question in the statement was asked out loud before it ever formed in my mind. It seemed my heart was speaking from my own wounded soul.* This was such a unique experience. It had not even dawned on me until I voiced the question out loud that the money could have been earmarked for an abortion. I told them that if I could go back in time and do it differently or if someone had warned my husband and me, maybe we would have another child today.

I shared with them that my husband and I have experienced God's love, grace, forgiveness, mercy and the truth of His gospel. We know we do not fully comprehend the goodness of what Christ did on the cross. For years, **I thought being a Christian was about my**

being good but God has shown me it is about how Good God is. He has shown me His goodness. How good He is to forgive me where I have fallen short and failed miserably. I also shared about what I see as real Christianity versus a "trying to earn one's forgiveness/ salvation" (Galatian's type) mentality. I talked with them for some time, and they seemed to listen. It was a peaceful conversation as I felt my heart pleading with them to hear the importance of what God was doing and warning. We parted with a congenial goodbye.

I drove away amazed with what had transpired. I pondered how losing what is valuable, even feeling bankrupt, has brought me to understand God's redemption. I prayed this couple would not have to experience such a loss to understand God's love and redemption.[4]

As I considered the experience at the restaurant, I realized that such an extraordinary encounter happened as a part of our normal life as we traveled to see my husband's elderly mother. God shows Himself in our daily lives and offers us ways to share the greatness of His ways and gospel with others.

When comparing this interaction at Firehouse in comparison with my experience of hearing the coughing man, (Chapter 2) I realized my heart, in both situations, was to share ***the treasure of Christ*** with all involved. Christ is my truest treasure but I have not known or been successful in sharing Him effectively often. I do not think I am alone. My heart is to allow the Holy Spirit to work through me when given opportunities to share. I am thankful the Lord keeps placing me in situations that help me to learn and grow. It is said that DL Moody, in his passion for saving souls, determined not to let a day go by that he did not share Christ.[5]

"I shall run the way of Your commandments, for You will enlarge my heart"
(Psalm 119:32 NASB)

"Above all else, guard your heart, for everything you do flows from it" (Proverbs 4:23 NIV)

I ask—the God of our Master, Jesus Christ, the God of glory—to make you intelligent and discerning in knowing him personally, your eyes focused and clear, so that you can see exactly what it is he is calling you to do, grasp the immensity of this glorious way of life he has for his followers, oh, the utter extravagance of his work in us who trust him—endless energy, boundless strength. All this energy issues from Christ: God raised him from death and set him on a throne in deep heaven, in charge of running the universe"

(Ephesians 1:20-21 MSG).

Prayer

Father God, we ask for a wide-open hearts, enlarged by Your Love (Psalm 119:32) and above all else help us guard our hearts for everything we do flows from our hearts (Proverbs 4:23). Help us know Christ as our treasure and share Christ as our treasure. May the good news of forgiveness be evident in our lives and shared with others passionately and with great love and care. May those that have been forgiven much, love much and share Christ much! Help us to run the way of Your commands and show others Your commands are for their good. Help us be wide open to You, Lord and guarded from the deceit and beguilement of the enemy. (2 Corinthians 11:3) Please protect us from wrong choices. May those planning on wrong actions, be turned back by your warnings and admit them to You, Lord for forgiveness. May we realize repentance is a gift and no longer deny, justify or hide in our sinfulness. "May we come to confess our iniquity and be sorry for our sin" (Psalm 38:18 ESV). Thank you for assuring us of Your forgiveness when we come to You in repentance (1 John 1:9) Enlighten the eyes of our hearts, Lord. May our mouths tell of Your wondrous works of salvation, Your might to a new generation, and Your power to all those that come. May we **be willing and determined to have a wide-open heart, enlarged but guarded above all else to love and share Christ as our greatest treasure.** In Jesus' Name, Amen [6]

Chapter Six

Confirmation of God's Mercy
Deborah

"He who conceals his sins will not prosper, but whoever confesses and renounces them will find mercy" (Proverbs 28:13 BSB).

"Jesus made the option of a new identity for all people in His redemptive work on the Cross. He was in the world reconciling us to God." [7]

Many of us have past self-centered sin-based decisions and actions that have caused deep pain. We cannot change the past but we can apply the Gospel to the past. But to do so, we have to acknowledge and bring these places to the cross of Christ. Sadly many try desperately to hide or live around "these places of past sin," some are places of "elephant sins."

In our lives the "elephant sin in the room of our lives was our abortion". It is our "past, very secret place of sin and shame". It was hidden from others for decades yet remained "the huge elephant in the middle of our lives".

If you read the beginning of this chapter, you might consider replacing any discussion of abortion with your own "secret sin" or "place of shame". If you consider your own personal "elephant sin in the room" or your own struggle, we pray you will come to know it can become **your own place of redemption**. ***The very thing that almost killed us, can be used by God to help us and others once we have had our own personal experience of Jesus, His Cross and Christ's redemption.***

I pray if you read on through our struggle and eventual victory, that God will use His Word and our witness to bring you to receive His forgiveness and freedom in a fuller measure or perhaps come to salvation, if you do not know Christ personally already. I pray you will move forward in your life in relationship with Jesus and having allowed the Lord to send "your own personal 'elephant' sin(s)" as far as the East is from the West, never to be counted against you (Psalm 32:2 and 103:12).

Coming to a place of knowing God's forgiveness and mercy helps us re-frame the past with His Grace! If you had an abortion or know someone that has had one or more and is struggling, perhaps some of this writing, and the post-abortive reference guide at the end of the book, will help.

Our hope is to help people be better equipped to understand and recover from their struggles and hardships from the place of our own now redeemed past. Once we know Christ, it is a place of beauty for ashes. (Isaiah 61:3) Also we hope to help those considering abortion to evaluate the enormity of the permanent consequences in this choice by sharing by our experiences, what we have learned.

Sharing from experiences can only go so far. The grief…the anguish, the things I have felt are too raw to write to the public: the letters we wrote to our baby still stagger me to a place of shock and disassociation. I could barely breathe; the fact is there are times that I have wanted to stop breathing. It is hard to live and move forward. I could not, if not for Christ.

My experiences of sexual abuses, occult abuse and abortion were like layers of wounds, deep within my soul. My reactions added to the depth of grief and agony. At times I felt dead. Even worse, if that is possible, alive but feeling worthless and in traumatic stress, emotionally unstable, feeling on or over the edge, misunderstood, misjudged, hopeless—feeling beyond God's grace and man's acceptance, triggered by many things, as a way of life. I lived feeling suicidal for many years. (For those who have experienced abuse, you may relate?) I knew suicide was what Satan wanted. This kept me from ever attempting it but the feelings were strong and at times relentless. It took God and consistent time in His Word to help me want to live, and fight to live. It was often a daily "choice". God showed me in Psalm 118:17 (ESV) "I shall not die, but I shall live, and recount the deeds of the LORD" or as the NLT v17b says: "I will live to tell what the LORD has done".

I know I would not be alive today but for Jesus! My family agrees. Jesus rescued me, loved me, forgave me, accepted me, healed me and became my best ally, and my life. He taught me His Gospel and its Good News and hope! He helped me feel safe to share with Him my real feelings. I confessed to Him my bitterness, anger, hate, rage, vengefulness, self pity, resentments, depression and the many other feelings and forces so common with abuses and abortion. He taught me to be real with Him, to admit my feelings and if and when I sinned, to run to Him to repent and allow Him to change me: to apply the Gospel to myself!

His Spirit of Truth continues to filter out the layers of lies and lead me into greater truth and freedom (John 8:31-32 & 16:33).

Our abortion is the blight of our lives. We could not tell of it if we did not believe and live in the love of God and the assurance and experience of the Gospel. We believe we are being directed by the Lord to share what we have shared.

Many readers may not feel led to share as we have. That is A-ok. My friend Grace reminded me "*that people may not share to this level of vulnerability for many reasons, not the least of which would be hurting people they love. But to share **as God leads** with discretion as to what to share and how to share it, with people God has put in one's life or will put in one's life is the goal. Jesus deals with us individually. Some things need to be kept private. They are not meant for discussion with others. Sometimes telling details of a season of dark sin would not edify the hearer and is not what God would want or lead. The hope is for believers to have a willingness to share their journey of God's love, mercy and forgiveness of sin and failure as GOD LEADS. Sharing our journey's or reading about someone else's journey can help others walk out their own.*"

Further, Grace wisely warned me to share this: *"Sometimes not disclosing something is about protecting someone else from harm, it's not about hiding one's own sin. It feels very much like you are asking everyone to be willing to be transparent in the same way you have been; encouraging everyone to do likewise can be difficult for others to accept."*

We want to make clear we are *not* pressuring anyone to share as we have!

We hope to encourage all believers to really pray and seek the Lord and ask the Holy Spirit to make Luke 12:12 real to you. If you are led, get Godly trusted counsel and share only what The Lord leads in all testimony!

Sharing that you have been forgiven for your sin through Christ, His Gospel, is what is important! (see 1 Corinthians 15:1-4)

Again, pray and seek The Lord. Get counsel if you feel the need. Consider researching how to give Godly testimony and ask God for confirmation on how to share your testimony so you share as God would have you share. Be prepared to share as in 1 Peter 3:15:

*But in your hearts set Christ apart [as holy—acknowledging Him, giving Him first place in your lives] as Lord. Always be ready to give a [logical] defense to anyone who asks you to account **for the hope and confident assurance [elicited by faith] that is within you, yet [do it] with gentleness and respect**.(1 Peter 3:15 AMP)*

Our hope is to encourage readers to live true to sharing Christ as our treasure and the hope we have in Him.

Again, we share our story the way we have because we believe we are obeying The Lord. Also it is timely and needed in light of the fact sexual abuse (The Me Too Movement) and abortions are rampant in our society. Plus, occultism is a factor in our nation and world. Sometimes all of this is connected. It was for me! Forgiving others and being forgiven brings freedom. We want to help people apply the solution of the Gospel to their personal experiences of sin, especially those sins that are not usually, openly talked about. (In particular the "Elephant sins" in the middle of the room/church that so many seem to ignore.) Telling our story, (our elephant sins) we pray, will be a catalyst God uses to help people know God's Good News, His forgiveness for sin to help others in their journeys of faith!

The rest of this chapter is specific to abortion. We debated long and hard in prayer whether to put this section here or at the end of the book. It seems best to keep it here but readers are free to skip to the next chapter.

I believe this section flows with the rest of the book and shows the overall theme of the book. Thus, I will share about this challenging hot topic. To start, may we recognize there are many factors that play into the decision to have an abortion. As a result, talking with someone who is considering, or has had, an abortion can be very challenging. Prayer for the work of the Holy Spirit is needed.

An article in The Journal of Obstetrics and Gynecology reported a study that found a link between those who were sexually abused and those who also have experienced abortion, especially repeat abortion. [8]

{Considering this study, I would like to mention statistics that may relate and show the need for the gospel within inmate populations. While volunteering with Youth for Christ, Manatee County Coalition for Offender Rehabilitation and Re-entry provided a handout with these statistics: 96% of female inmates have been victims of SEVERE sexual or physical abuse. 96% of these women have drug and alcohol problems as a direct result of this abuse. 48% of these women spent their childhood in the Foster Care system. 76% have never received consistent therapy. 89% have children. 75% of children whose parents are offenders become offenders.}

The needs of people are great! Back to the subject of abortion:

One website reports that people are ***victims*** of abortion. [9](American Victims of Abortion Website. "Women have cited "social reasons," not mother's health or rape/incest, as their motivation in approximately 93% of all abortions."[10]). In June 2018, Jeffrey M. Jones reported a special series on Americans' attitudes toward abortion: 48% identify as pro-choice, 48% as pro-life. Half continue to say abortion should be legal in some circumstances. Slightly more say it is morally wrong than morally acceptable. [11]

Abortion seems to have divided our nation. There are many needs related. Foremost, forgiveness and healing are needed in exponential ways. For post-abortive men and women, real recovery can be mirage-like for some who have repeatedly heard about God's judgment for abortion but have not known about or relied on God's mercy for abortion. A question: has judgment been preached and written about, more than God's mercy?

The Lord's faithfulness to give me this interaction (Firehouse #1), with this couple brought new hope that the Lord would use my sad past, wounds, and failures to share what I have learned in experiencing sin's cost and the blessing of true repentance. The role of warning people, like this couple, is part of God's goodness.

Hopefully, my testimony could prevent the tragedy of abortion for others. Just as important, I pray my testimony would allow multitudes of post-abortive people to clearly hear of and come to know that the forgiveness and mercy of God for sin, especially abortion, is available through Christ.

The wonder of God's mercy is beyond my understanding in its greatness. The mercy I have received has been so incredible that I continue to stand amazed and in awe of His lovingkindness and goodness. The magnitude of realization of the fact I deserved judgment has increased the joy of the mercy God has poured out on me. In our seeing a need for mercy, we come to a place of awe. The danger of judgment is real. That danger felt real to me in my own life and when reflecting on my interaction with the couple in Firehouse #1. It seemed confirmed when, after leaving the couple, I arrived at the hotel. The clerk handed me the room key assignment to 911. I gasped in my heart and soul. That number and its symbolism holds the idea of judgment, to me. The 911 room assignment and the events at Firehouse brought a warning and words to mind.

In the book, *The Harbinger*, by Jonathan Cahn the judgment America deserves is discussed. Cahn wrote that America has "a tolerance for everything that is opposed to God" and then described how America compares to what happened to ancient Israel. Cahn wrote, "Ten years after removing prayer and Scripture from its public schools, the nation legalized the killing of its unborn. The blood of the innocent now stained its collective hands. Israel had sacrificed thousands on the altars of Baal and Molech. But by the dawn of the twenty-first century, America had sacrificed millions. For its thousands, judgment came on Israel. What then of America? … America is in danger of judgment." [12]

Thankfully, God's mercy can triumph over judgment. **The Bible's clear message is that God delights to show mercy and give forgiveness.** I believe the message to trump judgment is the great mercy of God! (Micah 7:8; Luke 15:20-24; Psalm 86:5; Exodus 34:6; Romans 9:23; Psalm 130:4; Luke 23:34; Matthew 1:21; Luke 1:77; Mark 2:17; Matthew 26:28; Isaiah 53:4-5; 1 John 2:12; Psalm 103; Isaiah 43:25; 1 John 1:9; Isaiah 55:7; Daniel 9:9 and many other verses!)

"For judgment is without mercy to one who has shown no mercy. Mercy triumphs over judgment" (James 2:13 ESV).

God's Word says mercy can triumph over judgment: this is great mercy and hope. The Lord does not want any to perish. (See 2 Peter 3:9 and 1 Timothy 2:3-4). When we repent and turn to the Lord, we receive true forgiveness for sin—even for abortion.

However, the more research I have done on abuse, abortion and occultism, the more I am convinced that we, as a nation, deserve judgment. (Remember, with repentance, God delights to show mercy!) The numbers of abortions are staggering and the statistics from post-abortion surveys are surprising. One survey found 70 percent of women who get abortions identify themselves as Christians. [13] "Over 40 percent of women who have had an abortion say they were frequent churchgoers at the time they ended their pregnancies and about a half of them say they kept their abortions hidden from church members, new LifeWay Research shows." [14]

If the many reports and statistics prove true in revealing how prevalent sexual immorality and abortion is among Christians and church going women there is much hypocrisy.

Sadly it is reported, …"thousands of professing Christians get abortions every year. This unsettling fact was recently reported all too smugly in the feminist magazine *Marie Claire.* The article, titled "The Secret Evangelicals at Planned Parenthood," announced, "They may demonize the health clinic in public, but throngs of young Christian women are patronizing it in private for birth control, preventative care, and yes, even abortions." [15]

The writer of the above article treats abortion as a viable solution, ignoring the fact that it takes an innocent life and saddles some women and men with a lifetime of grief and regret. Sanya Richards-Ross, five-time Olympic gold medalist, and an outspoken Christian, stated that she had an abortion just before the 2008 Games. Though her decision enabled her to capture Olympic glory, she called it "a decision that broke me, and one from which I would not immediately heal. Abortion would now forever be a part of my life." [16]

Abortion is probably the most politically charged medical procedure in American history. It's also fairly common. "About 3 in 10 U.S. women have one by age 45. Over a third of women getting abortions are white. Over half are 20-somethings. Almost half make incomes under the federal poverty level. Most are already mothers." [17]

A ministry to post-abortive fathers states: "More than 50 million fathers have lost children to abortion in the US alone, since 1973. That number is equivalent to the populations of California, Oregon, Washington, Wyoming, Nevada, and Arizona combined." [18]

We could camp on the ongoing epic numbers of abortion worldwide. The enormity of the death rate is staggering and holocaust-like daily! There is a website that literally shows the rate of abortions as they have occurred and are reported. [19] Watching the numbers go up is like being at a gas station pumping gas and watching the numbers go up as the fuel tank fills. However, if we were present at these abortions we would be seeing the blood flow! It is a nauseating, surreal experience to watch the numbers go up so quickly and realize the significance of each number! For instance, on this particular date, shortly after the noon hour, there were 1,450.7 abortions in the USA alone.

To make matters worse, depending on the reference and the stance of the organization, statistical studies report a wide variance in percentages of post-abortive women who report someone forced, coerced, or put pressure on them to abort. [20] If we were to include worldwide statistics, especially China's policies, and sex-trafficking abortion statistics, the "often forced abortion reality" would be undeniable to any reasonable non-biased individual. These numbers show *abortion is not always a woman's choice.* Sometimes she is abused or faces some other pressure or violence or "governing law". In crisis abortions like these where injustice and coercion seem to reign, God can still do miracles. His redemption can triumph and bring good from evil. Only God can do this and He promises to do so in so many places in His Word. God is the God of forgiveness and redemption. (Romans 8:28; Genesis 50:20; Psalm 103, Psalm 51, Psalm 32 and many other verses.)

Research has shown that a woman who is forced into an abortion or a man who has a mate that chooses an abortion against his desire, have a much harder time generally accepting the outcome of abortion and recovering from the trauma. Considering this, these women and men need a different and unique approach to healing. Also, even men and women who willing have chosen an abortion often, after the abortion, have great grief. [21]

The main point: worldwide there is a need for help for post-abortive men and women. The gift of God is Christ and His forgiveness of sin and is the first solution to this worldwide epic need.

This is the main theme of this book: we have, (there is), great sin but we have, (there is), a greater Savior, Redeemer, Treasure, therefore, we are to *be willing to share Christ as*

our greatest treasure! **Sharing Christ is caring about people and their eternal souls and leads to fulfilling the call of our lives through the great commission and works Christ prepared for us to do.**

Post-abortive reactions vary widely. Some men and women state that they have no grief. Some actually report that they celebrate their decision and are glad for "their choice" and its action. They say it was the right thing for them and they say that they do not have negative affects from the abortion. For others, grief, pain and regret can be debilitating and bring great despair. The negative effects for some are deep and destructive. Sometimes the negative effects eventually are health altering and life affecting.

The need for forgiveness may or may not be realized by the parties involved in the abortion initially, for years and for some, maybe not on this earth. (But, we believe that at some point after an abortion, for most, the reality of what was done will sink in. There will be an impact.) For many, regret or conviction will come. A need to repent and/or to seek forgiveness may follow. *The way that forgiveness might manifest itself* may be different, depending on the circumstances:

*It may be forgiveness is needed toward the one(s) who coerced. *It may be forgiveness in needed towards "churches or individuals" who have caused further woundings by judging, condemning, and not extending the message of forgiveness and mercy needed in recovery. *It may be that forgiveness is needed to forgive their partner or their self or some report that they feel they even need to forgive God. Each particular situation is unique. Asking for forgiveness from God and the aborted baby (an any other person involved) is usually the start to real forgiveness and healing.

I listened and highly recommend listening to an interview with John Piper and John Ensor with the famous rapper, Lecrae, about the pain and consequences of Lecrae's sexual abuse and abortion. The lyrics of his song *Good Bad and Ugly* are Lecrae's testimony of his abortion with his girlfriend. His confession brought forth his healing. The principle that **confession brings healing** has been true in our lives and is Biblically supported. **Our souls prosper in the forgiveness and mercy of God and the sharing of His grace!** Here are three quotes by these three men:

"Sometimes we try to bury our sins, but the healing process begins when we let them come to light." ~Lecrae

"The guilt and regret of abortion is the most common human experience of our generation." ~John Ensor

"The gospel teaches us how to live, but it also rescues us when we fail to live the way we are supposed to." -John Piper

In this interview, (footnote provides the link) John Piper recounts meeting with a man who performed abortions. The conversation between them was very surprising (*below, the statements of Piper with the abortionist is in the bolded section within the interview with Lecrae and Ensor).* It showed the thinking of the abortionist's wife about abortion and may reflect many women's view. Here is the full verbatim quote within the interview, written with permission:

John Piper: "Well, you are absolutely right that the health issues are a camouflage. That is a ruse. That is a cloud that is put up, because statistically giving birth to babies is safer than abortions. That's not going to play out. The socioeconomic issues, the lifestyle issues, the education issues, the "my future" issues, carry the day. [22]

And then there are some pretty sophisticated justice issues that are brought up. I mean, the most moving thing I ever experienced was **taking an abortionist out to lunch, named Bill Long, and prepared to tell him he is killing babies. He said: "I know I am killing babies." And I said: "So what do we need to discuss?" He said, "My wife insists that I do this for justice reasons." I said, "Explain." And he said: "Look. Two people have sex. Guy gets off scot-free. She's stuck with the baby. That's unequal and unjust. One way to fix that injustice . . . abortion."** It's a justice issue for many people. So that is how complicated it can get in the justification.

The health issues aren't really there. And beneath that is just really the man's issue. You can't walk away, we must not let that guy walk away. We don't say it is *your* problem; it's *the-two-of-you* problem. In fact, I was so moved just a few minutes ago when you were talking about your background you said "*we* had an abortion." I almost wanted to cry at the rightness of that statement. So, yeah, I think you are right on. The kinds of excuses that are brought up are generally not the issue." (quoted with permission) [23]

The issue of abortion covers a gamut of views of all kinds. I have found some that seem **reasonable considering the standpoint of what some women have suffered**: Some women believe that if "the right to choose" is taken away that man's oppression and control of women will increase. Some believe abortion is only about "the right over a woman's body": a woman's right to her own body is what is at stake...that it is a restricting woman's rights to take away "choice". (ie: Some are adamant that woman need the right to make their own decisions, that is all "choice" is about! And because that is it, it is not a tough issue). Some are still heart-broken for friends they lost to illegal abortion and some had no choice back then (before legalization) and feel slighted and pained at missed opportunities and want a chance or "a choice," for those coming behind them. Some have never thought that a woman could be forced into an abortion and wonder how a person could let themselves be forced. Some cannot fathom that it is **not** always a woman's choice. Some feel without the option of "choice" women will be forced to bear children and that is a different kind of forcing. Some believe abortion is a protection of a fetus from worse abuse as a child after birth (a possible life of misery) if a baby is born to inept or unfit, unprepared parent(s). Some believe it is financially or medically a necessity. There are all kinds of thoughts and rationale to the reasons why people are taking sides on this topic.

This book is NOT about taking sides. It is about building bridges of understanding and offering help to any wanting help to heal and recover from abortion. My heart aches for all the unfair awful things women (and men) have gone through. My heart is to help people find peace in their past sufferings. It is about helping people faced with a current pregnancy to really consider their decisions carefully. It is about **<u>not letting anyone be forced into an abortion</u>**...and to encourage people to seek help if coercion is attempted.

Again, some women regret having an abortion but others say they don't. The articles and statistics on "regret" versus "no regret" vary widely. Yet perhaps most might agree it is a hard choice to feel one has to make, to lose a baby and the life that would have been. Again, my **heart is to help ANYONE, male or female, who has had an abortion and is struggling with healing. This is my focus.**

With every abortion, forgiveness and healing is needed, whether all parties realize it or not. Only The Holy Spirit can bring conviction. John 16:8 (AMP) "And He, when He (The Holy Spirit) comes, will convict the world about [the guilt of] sin [and the need for a Savior], and about righteousness, and about judgment": (Some other verses to show The Holy Spirit brings conviction &/or that conviction is needed or has happened: Psalm 51:4; Romans 1:18-23; Romans 2:5; Acts 16:30; Acts 17:30; Ephesians 2:1-9; Hebrews 4:12-13; Luke 13:5, John 6:44; ...many verses...) I pray that we **<u>will be willing</u> to make Jesus the greatest treasure and the Cross of Christ the main boast of every service and life of each believer (Galatians 6:14; 1 Corinthians 2:2).** May we recognize that Christ alone can bring the truth to people who are battling with post-abortion regret. God offers forgiveness to us through the Cross. Understanding the greatness of His love and forgiveness enables us to receive and extend forgiveness to others and obtain real healing and recovery.

The Lord's Prayer (Matthew 6:7-13) where Jesus taught his disciples to pray states:

Forgive us the wrongs we have done as we ourselves release forgiveness to those who have wronged us. Matthew 6:12 The Passion Translation (TPT)

"And ***forgive us our debts, as we have forgiven our debtors*** *letting go of both the wrong and the resentment." Matthew 6:12 AMP*

All forgiveness is available through Christ. His gospel gives us hope. God's promise of always forgiving the repentant (see below verses) and bringing redemption is hope. (Romans 8:18, 8:28, Genesis 50:20)

"The wages of sin is death but the gift of God is eternal life" (Romans 6:23).

"And this is the real and ***eternal life:*** *That they* ***know you, The one and only true God, And Jesus Christ, whom you sent"*** *(John 17:3 MSG)*

"For God so loved the world, that he gave his only Son, that whoever believes in him should not perish but have eternal life. For God did not send his Son into the world to condemn the world, but in order that the world might be saved through him. Whoever believes in him is not condemned, but whoever does not believe is condemned already, because he has not believed in the name of the only Son of God. And this is the judgment: the light has come into the world, and people loved the darkness rather than the light because their works were evil (John 3:16-19 ESV).

"O Jerusalem, Jerusalem, the city that kills the prophets and stones those who are sent to it! How often would I have gathered your children together as a hen gathers her brood under her wings, and you were not willing!" (Luke 13:34 ESV)

Jesus is willing even for those that have killed to come be His, to gather them and be to them like a hen gathering her chicks under her wings, but the verse ends: **'you were not willing.' Would you not be willing to come (or share this great invitation to others) so forgiveness can be granted and safety in the presence of Christ realized?** The shadow of the Almighty God is an awesome place of refuge! God's great forgiveness is available. He longs for any who do not know Him to come to Him.

The "Firehouse 1" couple may have been fighting over "the choice of abortion". They may have gone ahead with an abortion even after my warning and discussion. But, be that as it may, God still offers forgiveness. The *scandalous* grace of God is the wonder working power of true love. God is incredibly merciful.

I am thankful for the opportunity God gave me to share with this couple. It gives me hope. I pray the Lord will use our deepest pains and sadness over our abortion to warn others of how they may feel after. It cannot be undone, once it is done. For us, that choice has been a horror and brought life-long pain and regret. Hopefully, our testimony can help others to choose life. If not, just as importantly, I pray our testimony will bless multitudes of post-abortive people to clearly hear of and come to know that the forgiveness of sin, and a clear conscience due to received forgiveness, even for abortion, is available through Christ.

"When God extends grace, he doesn't just go to the cabinet and grab some mercy and forgiveness. God is holy. His character requires Him to justly punish sin. And the just punishment for sin is wrath and death. We have to remember that although grace is a free gift to us, grace was not free. Punishment toward sin had to be carried out; the price had to be paid. And it was, on the Son of God-who perfectly kept the law of God-on the cross. Grace was not free, it cost Jesus everything."
~Matt Slick

"God's blessing through Christ, to me, who deserves His curse." ~CJ Mahaney

A prayer based on 3 John 1:2 NIV: "Dear friend, I pray that you may enjoy good health and that all may go well with you, even as your soul is getting along well." Our soul's getting along well is what most want. The grace of forgiveness is needed for our souls to truly prosper. After abortion many experience that this need is great. No matter how many have had abortions, our God can forgive and save and rescue all of them from the wages of sin if we will but turn to Christ in repentance. The Lord offers His great forgiveness. Our mission as believers is to show others the precious gift of God. His gift is Christ and his forgiveness and salvation. Christ paid our sin debt by purchase through His broken body and spilled blood on the cross and by His resurrection. Enabling our forgiveness cost Christ everything while He was on earth. We must tell the greatness of His forgiveness and love.

What will it take for us to break the silence that seems to be the norm inside many churches and begin heralding the good news? When will we begin to fully depend on the blood of the Lamb and live out Revelation 12:11 by giving our testimony (as God leads us, see explanation of this earlier in chapter), while leaving the results of our lives to the Lord?

God is loving, kind, and gracious. His character is only good. Jesus has done everything we need to be made right with His Father eternally, to grant forgiveness for our sins even though we deserve judgment. Anyone who refuses His mercy, His taking what we deserve, will receive what they have chosen-the absence of God. There is so much at stake. But ultimately God gives every individual "this choice": judgment or mercy!

Prayer

Lord of all, who became sin (2 Corinthians 5:20-21) so we could be forgiven, made right, reconciled to Your Father, please draw your people to Yourself. May you bring conviction and a need for forgiveness about in those who need this. May all who have experienced abortion that seek You, find that the weight of the reality of their sin is overcome by the power of God's love, mercy and grace. May any feelings of guilt, shame, or a need to be punished be taken away in Christ by His bearing that guilt, shame and punishment at the cross. May those who confess their sin find healing. May their repentance and renouncing of their sin bring the realization of the enormity of the love and forgiveness Christ pours out on them so that they know they are truly forgiven. May the truth of being washed, sanctified, justified in the name of the Lord Jesus Christ and by the Spirit of God be a truth known and experienced by those who have come to Jesus for forgiveness of sin, even that of abortion. May the truth of hope found in Scripture point us to Christ. LORD, may Your Church make Jesus and His Cross the main message. May boasting on Christ alone be lived out. May people gain understanding of the Gospel to bring them to have a personal experience of Christ and His Cross for themselves. May the truth that only in the cross is eternal forgiveness purchased for us through Christ. May we gain greater understanding and experience of the greatness of Your Love, LORD and Your Forgiveness and please assist us to receive and extend forgiveness to others. Cause us to live the way of the cross, being In Christ and In His Word: may wisdom and ongoing guidance of the Holy Spirit bring forth real revival and recovery. May we recognize that you, Lord, take pleasure in those who fear You and in those who hope in Your steadfast love. Fill us with your love which turns us from ourselves and our sin to Jesus. Make us a delight to those who choose to hope in the strength of your amazing grace. Thank You LORD that You delight to forgive and extend mercy! May all **be willing** to come to Jesus, know their hope is secured because of the blood of Christ shed for them. May we want You and honor You, Lord. May we commune with You daily and live out our salvation. May a clear conscience with relief from the burden of sin and guilt be fully recognized through the truth of the Gospel and the receiving of Christ in relationship. [24] Thank you Lord that you are not slack concerning Your promise,...but You are long-suffering to us-ward, not willing that any should perish, but that all should come to repentance" (2 Peter 3:9 KJV). Help us be devoted to prayer, being watchful and thankful. Help us pray for others, too, that God may open a door for Your message Lord, so that we all may proclaim the mystery of Christ. Help us pray that I may proclaim it clearly, as we should" (Colossians 4:2–4 ESV). In Jesus Name

Chapter Seven

Reflections
Deborah

"Praise the Lord, my soul, and forget not all his benefits-who ***forgives all your sins*** *...who redeems your life from the pit and crowns you with love and compassion, who satisfies your desires with good things" (Psalm 103:2, 3a,4,5a NIV Emphasis Mine)*

'To be a Christian means to forgive the inexcusable because God has forgiven the inexcusable in you.' As far as forgiving yourself is concerned, he wrote, 'If God forgives us we must forgive ourselves. Otherwise, it is almost like setting up ourselves as a higher tribunal than him." -C.S. Lewis

As I think about this Firehouse #1 encounter, I am so grateful for God's presence with me as He gave me courage to speak out. The encounter has a bitter side too though because ***it is never easy for me, or us, to admit to anyone that I've (we've) had an abortion or to share the circumstances surrounding this decision***.

We grieve to this day over the loss of our child. It hurts me and it hurts my husband. Yes, we are forgiven and have a clear conscience because of Christ, but we cannot bring our child back.

I have however promised God, and our child, that I would do all I can to make our child's death count for life; to count both physically and eternally. We honor our child's lost life by living and giving out the messages of God's Word and Gospel. The power of God for salvation is available and we share with any, with hopes they will believe. It makes our telling of our abortion worth the pain of sharing, because we are assured that the result might be that mercy can triumph. (We pray that our truthful witness will save lives.)

"A truthful witness saves lives" Proverbs 14:25a ESV (Praying our truthful witness will save lives.)

For us, the bad news of sin, the wounding and wages of sin, have been experienced in our lives. A PT Forsyth quote comes to mind: "First you have to know 'the despair of guilt' then you can appreciate 'the breathless wonder of forgiveness'". We have received the wonder of Christ, His greatest news, gifts and grace. Our Savior Jesus Christ has overcome the world--all sin and all its consequences. Terrible, awful, really bad sins were placed on Christ. Christ experienced the wrath and death we deserved. This is how mercy triumphed. We often come to know how good God is when we know how bad, bankrupt or broken we are and our need for God's goodness. It is then that we taste and see that God is good.

"Give the Lord a chance to show you how good he is.
Great blessings belong to those who depend on him!" (Psalm 34:8 ERV)

"Oh, taste and see that the Lord is good!
Blessed is the man who takes refuge in him!" (Psalm 34:8 ESV)

O taste and see that the Lord [our God] is good; How blessed [fortunate, prosperous, and favored by God] is the man who takes refuge in Him Psalm 34:8 (AMP).

Once we believe in Christ, we have entered into Christ and He has entered into us through His New Covenant. We are born again. Thus, Christ is at work in and through us to bring about good works. How thankful I am for the changes He has brought about in me. From my beginnings it is evident to me and those that know me, that God has moved in my life and has done miracles.

"Let your light shine before men in such a way that they may see your good works, and glorify your Father who is in heaven" (Matthew 5:16 NASB).

"You are the salt of the earth." (Matthew 5:13a NIV)

"You are the light of the world." (Matthew 5:14a NASB)

****

I want to be the light and salt Jesus commissions me to be. I want to bring forth His good works and do the good works that He has created me for and prepared for me to do (Ephesians 2:10). I do not want to live in hypocrisy. Are you with me? To do so, we as

Christians need to be true to Christ and share about God's grace and mercy and live honest by applying the real gospel to ourselves and the world.

For all of us that have chosen to sin, knowing it is displeasing to the Lord, there is good news. We cannot change our past but our past can be redeemed by God. Gospel success is to fully live in God's grace and mercy in our greatest failures. It truly is Good News and the power of God to salvation for any who believe. (See Romans 1:16.)

Some of us may have more in common with David from the Bible than we think. He had sinned: "The thing David had done displeased the Lord" (2 Samuel 11:27b NIV). The Lord considered what David had done to be evil (2 Samuel 11:27b HCSB). David did so, when he knew better. David initially tried to cover up his sin. It led to more sin. The cover up attempt was perhaps worse than the original sin. Yet, it took Nathan, by God's guidance, to show David the reality of his sins (2 Samuel 12:7-14).

I lament in my identification with David! My attempt to cover my past teenage "elephant" sin led to me being so afraid that "I would be found out by people"; that I foolishly did not recognize that God saw it all! In my attempt to cover my past sin, I sinned more! This is a crushing truth. I only share it because perhaps many of us have lived trying to deny, justify or go on as if "it didn't happen" or cover our sins as Adam and Eve, David, Saul and others have. It never works and always makes more of a mess! The realization that God sees it all, and that the offenses were against Him, were hard to really admit. Cover ups before an all-seeing God are not possible.

God's knowing and seeing but still loving me is staggering grace and receiving God's forgiveness and mercy: these are what has led me to love God more and more! His Gospel is convincing proof of His great love!

Yes, amazingly, God delights to show mercy! He is gracious and forgiving! God sent Nathan to David. Perhaps, God will use this writing as a warning, like Nathan gave to David, to some reader out there? David said, "Blessed [fortunate, prosperous, favored by God] is he whose transgression is forgiven, And whose sin is covered. Blessed is the man to whom the Lord does not impute wickedness, And in whose spirit there is no deceit. When I kept silent *about my sin*, my body wasted away, Through my groaning all the day long. For day and night Your hand [of displeasure] was heavy upon me; My energy (vitality, strength) was drained away as with the burning heat of summer. *Selah.* I acknowledged my sin to You, And I did not hide my wickedness; I said, "I will confess [all] my transgressions to the Lord"; And You forgave the guilt of my sin." *Selah (Psalm 32:1-5 AMP).*

Repentance is a gift to bring us to God's great forgiveness. See Psalm 51.

Our sins hurt us and others and are against God Himself. In 2 Samuel 12:7-9 NIV it is asked of David by the Lord: "Why did you despise the word of the Lord by doing what is evil in his eyes?"

The key to receiving forgiveness is first admitting our guilt. It is being convicted by the Holy Spirit that real repentance comes forth. Trying to hide, cover, deny or justify our sin just worsens our guilt. David admitted his sin (2 Samuel 12:13). He was heart-fully sorry as seen in his response of fasting and worship in real repentance. Psalm 51 is a result of his repentance. Forgiveness was granted by the Lord. God forgave David for this sin against the LORD and spared his life (v 13). But forgiveness does not take away the consequences of our actions and the cost of sin. David's child died. Sometimes the consequences are long lasting, even until or past the length of our life, as was the case in David's life.

Prayer

LORD, help us live honestly before You and drop our masks and all attempts to hide, cover, deny, ignore or justify our sin. Please bring conviction of the Holy Spirit. Help us repent and realize the gift of repentance. May those who believe in You find that YOU are the greatest treasure and experience You afresh. May we receive your forgiveness, mercy and grace. Please restore to us the joy of our salvation, and uphold us with a willing spirit. Then we will teach transgressors Your ways, and sinners will return to You. Thank You that You deliver us from blood-guiltiness, O God, O God of our salvation, and our tongues will sing aloud of your righteousness. O Lord, open our lips, and our mouth will declare Your praise" (Psalm 51:12-15 ESV). May we all realize that You, LORD, are the Greatest Friend and only Savior and Lord! Help us really receive and reflect and extend Your forgiveness in our daily lives, and if You so lead us, help us tell our testimonies by Your Spirit's wisdom. Help us be Your *people who are called by Your name and humble ourselves, and pray and seek Your face and turn from our wicked ways. Thank you that if we do this, then You will hear from heaven and will forgive our sin and heal our land" (2 Chronicles 7:14 ESV).* Help us **be willing** to live true to Your truth and grace, mercy, forgiveness, love and acceptance. Help us be faithful to You. In Jesus' Name, Amen.

Chapter Eight

Firehouse Chronicle #2
Deborah

"That which is born of the flesh is flesh [the physical is merely physical], and that which is born of the Spirit is spirit. Do not be surprised that I have told you, 'You must be born again [reborn from above—spiritually transformed, renewed, sanctified].' The wind blows where it wishes and you hear its sound, but you do not know where it is coming from and where it is going; so it is with everyone who is born of the Spirit" (John 3:6-8 AMP)

"For those who follow Jesus Christ, our message to the world must be clear. God transforms the heart and mind and we become his children and his ambassadors. Let us so live that we will never be accused of hate or indifference. But let us also know that compromising the truth is a serious blunder and ends up celebrating that which is not in the will of our Father. This is a painful tension for a believer. To be seen as rejecting a belief or a behavior is not the same as rejecting the person. But God helps us to carry that burden." -Ravi Zacharias

Firehouse Chronicle #2

As I was driving to a conference, I stopped for lunch at Firehouse. I was still in awe of remembering the amazing experience at the Firehouse that the Lord had orchestrated during my last road trip. I prayed, "Please do it again, what only You can do. Show up. Show me what to do or say. *I sure would love to have another experience like the last time...but that is asking a lot because it would be hard to improve on that experience."* I felt like a child, looking to my trusted Father. I remembered Jesus' encouragement to his disciples to become like little children in Matthew 18:2-3, reassuring me. I felt secured and desired to trust God. My anticipation was high for what God might do.

My sandwich was ready and paid for but I felt no leading to talk to anyone yet. Initially I thought the Lord had answered a "No." But as I exited the building, I felt the Lord led me to a woman at the sidewalk table. I had no idea what to say to her, so I made small talk telling her of the conference I would be attending. I shared a bit about the speaker. She had heard the name of the ministry leader but was unfamiliar with her ministry. Thus, she did not seem encouraged to talk. My approach seemed to fail and it seemed we were both uncomfortable. I felt like a dunce. The awkward conversation ended, and I kindly excused myself and walked away feeling ridiculous.

Practicing God's presence and desiring to receive guidance from Him can feel strange. It is like wading into shallow waves like a toddler unsure of each step but determined for the adventure of the big ocean that awaits. I wanted to swim in His grace and Spirit but was still learning with each step.

I got to my car and in my heart, I knew I had taken a nose dive into the sand. As I prayed in my discouragement, I felt the Spirit nudge me to go back and really talk to her. *What did I have to lose?* She was almost finished with her lunch. She looked at me puzzled, so first of all I wanted to assure her I was not some lunatic. Yet, I felt strange and unsure in attempting to hear and follow God's promptings. Let's face it, living for Jesus while living on earth seems a little crazy sometimes. Yet, the magnitude of Christ's indwelling, His love and presence is our born-of the-Spirit reality. I am in love with Jesus so I may as well take the risks, especially when He asks me to do something that I asked Him to show me in the first place.

"I am back again. I just felt the Lord wanted me to talk to you but I'm not sure what about yet." Embarrassed, I pressed on. I asked her if I could sit down. She said yes and that she had a few minutes before her conference call for work. I told her I had recently had an incredible experience at Firehouse on my last road trip and briefly shared what occurred. She said, "I have chills all over." She began rubbing her arms. I shared a bit of my story and more about why I was determined to travel a long distance to hear the speaker at this ministry conference. I expressed how, in some traditional church settings, I sometimes had not found encouragement, acceptance, and understanding. At this ministry I did though, and the messages were like personalized gospel teachings I so identified with. I told her how I had come to really know and experience Jesus and his love, forgiveness, and acceptance especially after a history of tragic early childhood sexual abuse and its recovery.

That was the connection.

Her face lit up and she said, "That is why you were compelled to talk to me. Just last week our daughter (in her 20's) told us for the first time that she had been sexually abused when she was eight years old by a family friend whom we had trusted to babysit her." I heard the pain in her voice and words. She then opened up and shared some of her daughter's story. The similarities of the betrayal, sexual abuse, and the fall out, especially of the hurtful responses from others, were staggering. I was surprised by but pleased with our instant understanding of each other and the unity of the Holy Spirit that we experienced in sharing these struggles from our lives. There were obvious differences too. Her daughter has been in a same sex relationship for years and almost "married her first partner" but is now in another relationship. She said her daughter had been a Christian little girl before the sexual abuse. She said, "I pray every day for her but have had to let her go." (I think what she meant "to let her go" was to let her live the lifestyle she is living while still loving, accepting and praying for her. This mom's unconditional love and acceptance of her daughter, to me, seemed deep and real.)

Some of the devastation, pain, and heartache this mother felt for her daughter and the pain and sorrow both she and her husband have endured was shared. She said she felt nothing but judgment from their spiritual community. She expressed how hurt and betrayed she felt by the words and attitudes from many loved ones, even in their church family. She shared how it was worsened by the fact that at one time they had been very close knit with and supported by this group. She shared how as a mother of an only child she felt like a failure and how she blamed and shamed herself for her daughter's situation. Feelings of inadequacy, deep pain, and a desire for relief and support were expressed.

She talked of giving up attending church and how her faith had been impacted due to the onslaught of negativity and wounding. She shared freely and openly as I had done. I shared about God's love and forgiveness. I hoped my words would be helpful supports and hopeful encouragements to her. I felt that we had a very special fellowship and that God had been honored. It seemed we both went away blessed by the interaction.

Free of masks, it was a true gospel moment. God had answered my prayer.

We parted ways, and I was awed, rejoicing and glad I had obeyed the promptings I had received. I kept thinking of what I would have missed if I hadn't obeyed.

It felt like redemption. For God to use the worst events of my life to help others is like a seal of approval for me that the Lord is bringing about and confirming the ministry He has for me with post sexual-abuse families. The Lord was showing me His gospel works for every soul. I had been so stuck for so long, but as I have believed and lived in Christ's forgiveness, I have been getting spiritually healed. He is allowing me the opportunities to reach out and help those burdened and wounded by the judgments of others, like I was and sometimes still am. [25]

Some things that I have learned since that interaction that may have been helpful to this mother: 1. There are many articles and statistics linking sexual abuse with the LGBTQ rate of increase. (See Endnote #25) The information in the book referenced in Endnote #24 could have been hopeful to her. 2. References/referrals can be beneficial. [26]

Victims and their families need help in the recovery from abuse. I would have liked to have assured her more of the good job she was doing: of continuing to show her daughter unconditional love and support. I did share with her the sorrow (and need for repentance in many churches) for the treatment she, her husband and daughter have received from "Christians". It is so sad her family and daughter experienced such unlove, judgments, rejections, self-righteousness, etc. At the time of their greatest need of love, understanding, compassion and supportive acceptance they received just the opposite and they were sorely wounded. This seems to be the case and true of many in similar situations that interface with "Christians". It was often the case in my life. How are we representing Jesus Christ?

"For he has rescued us from the dominion of darkness and brought us into the kingdom of the Son he loves" (Colossians 1:13 NIV).

"Therefore, as God's chosen people, holy and dearly loved, clothe yourselves with compassion, kindness, humility, gentleness and patience. Bear with each other and forgive one another if any of you has a grievance against someone. Forgive as the Lord forgave you. And over all these virtues put on love, which binds them all together in perfect unity" (Colossians 3:12-14 NIV).

"Let the peace of Christ rule in your hearts, since as members of one body you were called to peace. And be thankful. Let the message of Christ dwell among you richly as you teach and admonish one another with all wisdom through psalms, hymns, and songs from the Spirit, singing to God with gratitude in your hearts. And whatever you do, whether in word or deed, do it all in the name of the Lord Jesus, giving thanks to God the Father through him" (Colossians 3:15-17 NIV).

Prayer

LORD, help us love others as you have loved us. Teach us to clothe ourselves with compassion, kindness, humility, gentleness and patience. Help us bear with each other and forgive one another. Help us put on love, which binds them all together in perfect unity (Colossians 3:12-14). Please help us be supportive and without judgment or criticism towards a parent like this mom and a daughter like this daughter. Help us live with caring, thoughtful consideration, insight and love in helping others bear the burdens they carry (Galatians 6:1-2). Help us live the Gospel to families struggling to help someone who has suffered sexual abuse, and all associated wounds, pains and sorrows. Help us recognize that many are cumbered with a load of care. Help us take others to the Lord in prayer. Help us provide resources and referrals and LISTEN with CARE and LOVE to comfort and uphold others. When hearts are fragile and sometimes broken please help us to infuse hope, encouragement and strength. Help us to really pray…love unconditionally…know when to speak and when to be quiet and pray. Help us be patient and not push or bully in any way. May God's wisdom in every communication and contact be evident. Help us love people where they are and seek to understand their feelings and heartaches in caring, kindness and compassion. Lord, help us to be patient and to be led by the Holy Spirit. May we be passionate to proclaim the extraordinary message of Your rescue. Help us trust You more and share You and Your Truth to bring people to understand how precious Jesus is and how He knows and cares. Help our past be in line with the future Jesus offers us through His resurrection. We are truly made-new creations. Help us **be willing to live new and true to Christ. Help us proclaim and live John 3:16-17 more effectively** please, Lord. In Jesus' Name, Amen. [27]

Chapter Nine

Two Kingdoms
Deborah and Richard

For I know that my Redeemer and Vindicator lives, And at the last He will take His stand upon the earth (Job 19:25 AMP).

And the seventh angel sounded; and there were great voices in heaven, saying, The kingdoms of this world are become the kingdoms of our Lord, and of his Christ; and he shall reign for ever and ever (Revelation 11:15 KJV).

There are two kingdoms: The Kingdom of God/Heaven and the kingdom of this world. To enter the Kingdom of God we must have a childlike faith in Jesus Christ as our Lord and Savior. At times, living this childlike faith may cause us to appear foolish according to the kingdom of this world. Satan, as the "head" of the kingdom of the world, (for now), works to steal, kill, and destroy (John 10:10). Satan sows lies and his ways are always contrary to the will and authority of God. The networks that he weaves are always webs of deceit — webs to divide, bring fear and a lack of understanding. Satan's plan is a frontal, all-out attack on the gospel. He plants seeds of doubt in our hearts and minds, in so many ways —using ideas and emotions that will cause division. It seems that his approach is three-pronged: 1) he does not want us to believe that God even exists—a strategy that seems more prevalent today. Satan wants us to focus only on the material— the things that we see and touch. He tells us that there is nothing else, so our lives should be focused on the material and using those things to satisfy our wants and desires. 2) even if we believe that God exists, Satan wants us to think that God is withholding good from us and keeping us from being the god of our own life. He never wants us to read God's Word or have a relationship with our

Heavenly Father, because the truth would set us free. 3) Satan does not want us to live by the overcoming power of the Cross of Christ! In Christ's finished work on earth by his death, resurrection, and ascension we have been given access to God the Father and the Holy Spirit indwells us even while on earth. God's kingdom is within believers of Christ (Luke 17:21).

Satan could not use the first approach with Adam and Eve because they knew God. Unfortunately they did not know God well enough to fully trust God and believe in His good and loving intentions. This should be a constant reminder and warning to those of us who also believe in God. We need to always be on guard against the lies.

The "hotpoint" issues in our society today are all fundamentally driven by these lies from Satan. Satan's plan is for us to think that this world is all there is and that our short time of life should be spent fulfilling our dreams and desires. He wants us to look within ourselves alone to know what is best for us and then to follow what we feel. As gods, we determine what is right and wrong, good and evil, in our lives.

But **if** the God of the Bible is real, then we have His Word that Satan is a liar, even the Father of Lies. Satan wants to destroy us - not just physically but spiritually as well. And **if** the God of the Bible exists, then we know that He created us. He knows us better than we could possibly know ourselves. In creating all that exists, His knowledge and power are greater than we can possibly imagine. Further, He tells us and shows us that He loves us deeply and wants the absolute best for us. **If** the God of the Bible exists, He offers us the opportunity to have a relationship with Him, and He makes it clear how that relationship can exist - namely through Christ. In this relationship with God, we can have hope and rest; neither of which are available from the Kingdom of this world. **If** the God of the Bible exists, we know that our life on this earth is not all there is. God offers a life of eternal blessing, fulfillment and purpose in the New Heaven and New Earth that He will establish and in which He will reign.

So **if** the God of the Bible exists, why wouldn't we want to follow the directions that He gives us for our lives? Why would we possibly think that we could know better than God? Why wouldn't we trust the One who has been Good and Faithful since the very beginning?

Adam and Eve lost the kingdom of God within them because they did not trust God and believe what God said, at the Fall (Genesis 3). Christ reversed the Fall at the Cross. We, as New Covenant believers have the Kingdom within us through the Holy Spirit's indwelling! We are to live as more than conquerors! (Romans 8:37)

In taking a step of faith and sharing with others, we should know that the lies of Satan are really the foundational issue in every discussion. These lies are at the core, every time. The God of the Bible has the answers to all of our questions. There is Truth and He wants us to know the Truth and live by the Truth. The God of the Bible helps us to understand our origin, our meaning, our morality and our value. The Kingdom of this world only offers hopelessness and empty answers. So, we should always remember what Peter urges in 1 Peter 3:15 (ESV): always being prepared to make a defense to anyone who asks you for a reason for the hope that is in you; yet do it with gentleness and respect.

Satan's lies and schemes are evident in our culture and churches. The grace, truth, and love that are essential to living the gospel to those who don't know Christ are often woefully absent.

At times, hate, judgments and prejudices are prevalent in the churches. At other times The Word of God is not upheld as leaders and church members live unchecked and unaccountable, with all types of sinful behaviors. There seems a lack of both knowing and obeying God's Word and therefore being able to lovingly and effectively share it with others.

I know personally how difficult life can be to recover from sexual abuse and the fall out of its related struggles. Often the members of LGBTQ have a history of sexual abuse. [28] [29]

So often instead of helping victims, judgments and shame are poured out on them. It is terribly sad. At one point, I was like the daughter in Firehouse Chronicle #2 in many ways. God brought me out, helped me, and healed me. God can do miracles. He can even use judgmental people to grow us in grace, truth, compassion, and insight.

This mother at the Firehouse was hurt deeply by people in her church. This is a recognition that the two kingdoms are battling even in our lives and in all people professing to know Christ. Unfortunately, we all can bring our own narrow viewpoints and cast judgments in interactions with others, instead of allowing the Holy Spirit to guide us. This is critical when we are witnessing and sharing with others. We need to be earnestly praying and seeking God's guidance in these situations. There is God's reward in our seeking Him (Hebrews 11:6).

Jesus said He overcame the world, (John 16:33) that His kingdom has come (Matthew 12:28; Luke 17:21) and yet the coming of the Kingdom is still future (Luke 19:11-12). Jesus said His kingdom is not of this world. (John 18:36-37) There is a mystery to the Kingdom. Secrets of the Kingdom are given throughout the Bible. One thing we can be sure of even when it seems like evil is gaining strength on earth: Jesus is Victor; He has already overcome and His Kingdom will endure and reign and rule this earth. Jesus is the only Worthy One! The Lion of the tribe of Judah, has triumphed. He is able to open the scroll and the seven seals. (Revelation 5:5) Reading Revelation 5 tells us of God's amazing victory to redeem the earth! What Jesus did at His first coming gives His people all they need to advance His Kingdom on earth. We as believers need to live as "**over-comers**" in the world through the finished work of Jesus Christ, because of His death and resurrection and ascension! We need to share the great work of Christ as the way to overcome the world, flesh and devil! Ultimately, there will only be one Kingdom, and those In Christ are blessed to be members.

Prayer

Heavenly Father, teach Your people how to live by Your Kingdom. Thank you, Jesus, for enabling this Kingdom to come to us by paying our debt of sin in full and sending the Holy Spirit to indwell, comfort and lead us who believe. Help us live worthy of The Worthy One, Beholding The Lamb of God. Work through us to share with others so that they may experience the greatness of Christ and know their sins are forgiven. Help us recognize the pain and the pasts of others: we often do not know what other people have lived through. Remove from us any pride or feelings of superiority. Lord, help us repent of any narrow-mindedness, (even seen with close disciples of Christ in John 4 with the outcast Samaritan woman), and even hate or prejudice that infects and brings divisions and woundings. Help us realize that victims of crimes and/or abuses are often wounded and believing things about themselves and others that are not true. They are doing what they know to survive. Help us to be compassionate and caring. Help us speak truth and hope with grace and love! Help us to live from the indwelling Holy Spirit. In Isaiah 11:2 we are told that the Spirit of the LORD shall rest upon him, (the stump of Jesse), the Spirit of wisdom and understanding, the Spirit of counsel and might, the Spirit of knowledge and the fear of the LORD. Since we are IN Christ, Lord, help us to show Your Spirit's rest in us by Your wisdom, understanding, counsel, might, knowledge. May we respect You, Lord. Through the Spirit of the LORD may we extend grace to people who are different from us. Lord, help us depend on You and know Your adequacy is accessible to us. Help us live from Your Spirit. Please speak this over us as Your people, LORD: *"This is the word of the LORD unto Zerubbabel (us, LORD), saying, Not by might, nor by power, but by my spirit, saith the LORD of hosts." LORD, we need YOU! LORD, You know we are in a trying situation, and need special encouragement from You LORD God; and here it is: Not by might, (of our own), nor by power, (authority from other people), but by Your Spirit - the providence, authority, power, and energy of the Most High. In this way shall Your temple be built; in this way shall Your Church be raised and preserved."* (This prayer in italics, is using the Clarke's Commentary on the Bible for Isaiah 11:2.) In Jesus' Name, Amen.

Chapter Ten

The Inner Battles and Outside Wars
Deborah and Grace

"Blessed are the pure in heart, for they shall see God" (Matthew 5:8 ESV). "You're blessed when you get your inside world—your mind and heart—put right. Then you can see God in the outside world (Matthew 5:8 MSG).

"And there came in my life a vivid sense of having experienced the Atonement...with a consciousness of having the complete answer to all my difficulties and sins....the doctrine of the cross became a great reality for me.... a simple talk personalized the Cross for me that day, and suddenly I had a poignant vision of the Crucified. I began to see myself as God saw me, which was a very different picture than the one I had of myself..." Frank Buchman story in book Absolutely Sober, p 22-25)

The two kingdoms affect all of us on a personal level. So much of the battle of the mind and heart is a very real spiritual battle, with a very real enemy seeking to deceive us. I pray that this book will be used to call believers to see the need for, and be willing to live and speak, the truth in a way that extends to the world the very same love, truth, mercy and grace that we received from Christ and want to extend to others.

Christ met us "back there, in our past" and has brought us "to where we are now". Thus, it is critical so that we might see ourselves as we were, and as we are now, in light of Christ's Cross and His grace over us. John 13:3 states that Jesus Himself knew where he had come from and where he was going. For the sinless Son of God, Jesus' knowing where he came from and where he was going, had everything to do with God's perfect plan for Him as Savior of the World. His knowing enabled Him to do His Father's Will in all things, to include enduring the Cross. Thus, because of Jesus, we have a past that can be changed for good, no matter what we have done if we enter in and have a personal experience of Christ and His Cross. "Where you come from, and where you are going" is an extremely important consideration in our daily walk.

We can all look back at our own lives and see lifestyle choices we regret. Childhood pain, abuse, or trauma can trigger the kind of pain, loneliness, and decision making that pushes us toward various behaviors. As Christians, when we see our lives from the lens of the Cross, our life changes.

While we were still editing and finishing this book, I asked a close friend, Grace, to preview it. She was the first reader. Just hours after she had finished reading, she wrote some thoughts she had about her feelings as a child and young adult. I asked my friend's permission to share her writing. I hope it will be as precious for you as it was for me. What she shares about herself, perhaps may be true of all of us. Here is what Grace wrote:

"When God spoke to Adam and Eve after the fall, he asked them two questions: "Where are you?" and "Who told you that you were naked?" (see parts of Genesis 3:9-11 ESV)

These questions created room in my heart to see my own life from God's perspective. He has seen all of my life, that reality became the starting place for me to begin to see the truth about myself.

Even as a young person I sensed that I was covering up who I was inside. I've known what it feels like to be in hiding. I didn't want people to really know me. I wanted them to only know who I wanted to be. I wanted to be good. I wanted to be kind. I wanted to be smart. I wanted to be beautiful, and I wanted to be loved!

I thought that if anyone knew that person living down deep inside of me, they wouldn't love me. I felt unworthy of love.

I have lived a good part of my fifty-plus years trying to be the person that would be worthy of love by meeting the expectations of others, by being the good child, by being a good friend, and by doing good for others. I thought that by being someone others would approve, I would be worthy of love.

I knew that anger lived inside of me. I had anger for the things that had happened to me as a child as well as an adult. I had anger that I wasn't protected or loved in the way that I should have been. Even more so, I had anger at myself for never being good enough.

I knew in my head that God loved me. I knew that he sent his Son Jesus to die for me. I believed that was true, and I held onto it in my heart. But even though I knew it was true, I didn't live that way. I learned to live a life of performance.

I had many good teachers in this area of performing. My mom was one of my key performance coaches. She was great at showing her children what it looked like to be perfect on the outside. We all lived in her perfect world.

She was hiding her own childhood pain because she was raised by a mentally ill mother. She was the youngest of eight children whose religious upbringing was all about performance. No one told her that she was naked. She wore those perfectionist clothes very well. She almost looked perfect. At least, we thought she did.

My father also wore protective clothing. He was a pastor who hid behind his role as shepherd to the flock of all the hurting, naked people. He lost himself playing that role. He might have forgotten the truth that he was also naked before God, even though most people saw him as a well-dressed man of God. His childhood would remain his own secret.

Recently, I was on an airplane. I was thinking about my life's journey. The journey of our lives includes everywhere we have been and often determines where we are going. They say that the past doesn't determine your future. I think it plays a big role in our future. We have to know where we have been to see where it is we are headed. Sometimes, our life needs a new direction, these were the thoughts I was having as I sat in my airplane seat. As I waited on this airplane and looked around me, I saw all the people on this plane and the clothes they were wearing. I had an awareness that underneath their clothing was their naked true self. And underneath my covering was my naked true self. I wondered if all the other naked people knew that Jesus could see their nakedness.

Did they know that nothing was hidden from Him?

Did they know He knew all about them? Did they know He loved them?

Then suddenly, like a bolt of lightning, I became aware that He could see me in my nakedness. He could see who I really am. Even more astonishingly, He still loved me. He didn't want my performance. He didn't want my good appearance. He didn't want the nice clothes of good behavior that I was wearing. He wanted the real me. He wanted the authentic me. He wanted all of me —both the good and not so good parts of me. He wanted me to know how much He loved me, and how He had died for me. He wanted me to know how His death had given me new clothes to wear — not clothes of performance, not clothes of self-righteousness, but His clothes.

I no longer needed to wear clothing that didn't fit, clothing that could not cover my shame and guilt. I now could wear the clothing that His love and grace provides. They are His robes of righteousness that now belong to me. He dressed me in them, and it wasn't because I had been good. It was because I had been my true naked self that admitted who I really was — all of who I was.

I can be my naked self. I can be my truest self because He already sees and knows everything about me, yet He loves me. I understand now that I am worthy of love. I am fully known and loved fully.

In conclusion, The two questions asked of Adam and Eve following their original sin in Genesis 3:9-11, "Where are you?" and "Who told you that you were naked?" are questions that gave me a deeper understanding of my own journey.

Asking myself these two questions not only helped me to see myself as I am, but more importantly to understand how God knows me completely. I am utterly naked before Him.

Are you aware of your nakedness? He only wants to clothe you in his righteousness because He loves you. He wants us to bring all of our truest selves — both our strengths and our weaknesses — to find forgiveness and restoration that He alone has provided. Do you want Him to cover you with clothes that will never wear out and provide for you the deepest need you and I have — the covering of His great love for you? He's here, and He says, "Come."

"But God shows His love for us in that while we were still sinners, Christ died for us" (Romans 5:8 ESV).

I wrote these reflections of my own life journey immediately after I finished the reading of this book. I hope it will encourage those who struggle to know their own true identity. You are loved by the very God who not only knows you but created you to know Him.

My **prayer** for all of us is that we will find His love reflected in each of our lives as we live the life He has given each one of us: "To know that the life we have is meant to be lived for an audience of One. The One who truly knows and loves us."

Grace.

Thank you Grace! I love that God loves us even when He sees us as we truly are!

It is reassuring that The Lord pursued and went after Adam and Eve in their sin and hiding and trying to cover their nakedness and shame. He loved them there and provided for them and saw their naked true selves. He knew them infinitely better than they knew themselves. He forgave them and made atonement for them and walked again with them but in a different place and in a different way. Sin does cost us.

But God's mercy and goodness are our hope.

Now, I would like to introduce our friend, Sophia. She will share some of her story. We pray that together by the Holy Spirit we will all be better enabled to affect our generations, culture and families instead of letting them affect us. Thank you for reading and we pray it will be a "soul prospering journey" for you. God Speed!

Chapter Eleven

Wrong Paths and Dark Places

Sophia Asah

My husband said he could see where I got my sense of adventure from, the first time I brought him to my old childhood home. Our home had a lot of personality, set upon five acres, surrounded by trees and nature, and across from a spring-fed lake. I grew up exploring those woods and dreaming of endless possibilities. It was sweet, fun, and innocent. My dad loved to build. He built a giant playground that included not one but two playhouses, a tall slide, monkey bars, seesaw, and a trampoline, which my uncle bought for me. My mom was extremely attentive to me: read me book after book, took me to gymnastics practice, and made sure I knew when my tests were in school so I was prepared.

It was a wonderful life until my teenage years, when anxiety, insecurity, and my parents' divorce led me down a wrong path and into dark places: a drug addiction, homosexuality, rape, confusion, torment, suicidal thoughts, and a host of other issues. I believe all of this was the catalyst that eventually led me to God, healing, and redemption. My story is the story of salvation, of a journey through addiction and homosexuality, of support I received, and of the lessons I learned through healing and victories.

I hope you find what you are looking for in my story, and if you don't, keep praying and researching.

The Wrong Path

I was interested in, curious about, and attracted to boys, but I didn't know what to do with my awkward emotions and the one time I asked my mom what a BJ was, she reacted with shock and embarrassment. Her vague explanation left me with the impression that there was something bad, even dangerous, about sexual things and that was that. Nothing else was said and I somehow stayed away from promiscuity in middle school and it (mostly) seemed to stay away from me.

At twelve, I began to struggle emotionally and hormonally. I never told my parents or anyone else of my internal anxiety or struggles. I had occasional patterns of suicidal thoughts (for no apparent reason) and had started drinking at parties with older friends that had invited me. I even started using drugs. I had always been a straight-A student and had many friends. I was a cheerleader and never got into trouble (except talking too much in class). But my curiosity, passion for adventure, and desire to be free and unrestrained (with a little rebellion mixed in) led me to lie to my parents and do the things that the older, popular kids were doing.

I think I got sick the first time I drank, but I remember it being fun and an escape from anxiety and internal stress. It's a little foggy now, and I'm not sure I can articulate all that was going on, but it almost seemed like a carrot was dangled in front of me, and I followed it blindly. I started hanging around a different set of kids and I was introduced to cigarettes and weed and pills, and topics like bi-sexuality and promiscuity.

I was fourteen or fifteen when I heard guys talking about how they liked it when other girls kissed each other and hooked up. To them it was considered cool, something they liked (or lusted for). I really wanted to be accepted by them, and I desperately wanted to be in the *in crowd.* I remember hearing about two girls who "hooked up." I was sort of friends with them and started fantasizing about kissing one of them. One night while we were drunk, we made out. I liked it. It didn't continue, and I didn't hook up with any other girls during my high school years, but the seed had been planted. I never talked about it to anyone.

Dark Places

One day my dad said he wasn't happy with my mom. They are amazing parents and good people, but I don't remember them having much affection for one another. There was constant animosity between them, but it never occurred to me they would ever split up; it wasn't even on my radar. But the week after Dad said he wasn't happy with Mom, his bags were packed, and he walked out of the door. No explanation was made, but he said that he still loved me, he wasn't leaving me, and he would still be in my life. I think this was supposed to reassure me, and I tried to believe it was going to all be okay, but I was devastated. That was a major point of breakdown in my life, my view of men, and my acceleration in drugs. I was a Daddy's girl; losing him was not something I felt I could handle.

My reactions were, "*Men! I don't need them!*" This internal vow immediately put up a wall between me and men for a long time. I chose to protect myself by taking on a strong and tough exterior because I was terrified to face my feelings and shattered heart.

My mom saw me turn cold like a light switch just turned off, and I told her to leave me alone. If I was going to get through high school, that's how I was going to deal with it. Logically, I told myself to suck it up because many kids' parents were divorced or worse, dead. I reasoned that I still had them and they loved me. But I didn't know how to deal with the pain. My intentions were to grin and bear it. But instead, I turned to drugs even more.

I became obsessed with getting high and finding more drugs. I had totaled two vehicles and had an overdose by the age of fifteen, but my denial, good grades, and academic scholarship fooled me into thinking I had everything under control. It wasn't until I graduated and was given freedom as an adult to do what I wanted that my addictions and lifestyle got *way* out of hand.

I did things I never thought I'd do. I did things I never even *heard* of people doing. I was not built for the street life, but there I found myself, doing a lot of drugs, sleeping with a lot of men I barely knew—and even with other women. I was raped a few times and that was awful, but not too much worse than the regular feeling I had when I was with the men I gave my body to. Deep down, I didn't really want to be doing it, but the drugs intensified my sexual desires, and I wanted sex and even got drugs in exchange for it. I also felt obligated to give them what they wanted. My physical body was a tool that gave me some sort of value.

Even though my conscience told me "no" many times, I didn't have the strength to say "no" to sex with those men. My conscience was not strong enough.

Paul explains my situation well in his letter to the Ephesians, "So I tell you and encourage you in the Lord's name not to live any longer like other people in the world. Their minds are set on worthless things. They can't understand because they are in the dark. They are excluded from the life that God approves of because of their ignorance and stubbornness. Since they no longer have any sense of shame, they have become promiscuous. They practice every kind of sexual perversion with a constant desire for more" (Ephesians 4:17-19 GW).

People talk about morality and how it's important to have a strong moral compass, but what happens when your mind has become darkened and your moral compass is tainted or twisted? I found that my conscience wasn't enough. Later, I discovered that my morality needed to be strengthened and reinforced by my parents and by the Word of God.

Everything was a mess. My identity was shattered. My life was set on the fires of hell, and it wasn't until I ended up in jail that I began to unravel the mess I'd made.

Chapter Twelve

Encountering God
Sophia Asah

When I was nineteen, I was driving back from a probation meeting and was considering driving my car off the road into the trees so I could end it all. Instead, I looked down and there on the floorboard was a tape, which one of my drug dealers must have left there because no one else rode in my car. It was called *Divine Revelation of Hell.*

Before I tell you this story of my revelation in hell, I want you to know that my intentions are not to scare you, exaggerate, or fabricate drama. I actually left this entire story out until I finished writing. This story is very personal to me and not something I've shared with many people. But it came to my mind to add it because this experience became the foundation that led me to Jesus and eventually walk out of homosexuality. It was the beginning, the start, of my journey to live for God and not for myself.

I had heard of the word *hell* but had no idea what the word *revelation* meant. I wasn't raised in church, and we never talked about God. I only remember hearing the gospel one time at a Baptist Church that I visited because a friend invited me. At that church, they told me that Jesus died to save me from my sins and that I could be saved, which sounded like a good idea. *Who wouldn't want that?* So, I raised my hand to be saved but nothing happened because I didn't believe it in my heart: it was more of an intellectual idea. However, that experience planted a seed that I believe was watered shortly after I listened to the tape in my car.

In the car that day, I looked at that tape with curiosity and paranoia. I didn't want to even touch it, and yet I had nothing to lose. I picked it up and stuck it into the tape player.

A lady's voice began describing hell in vivid detail. She said hell is an actual place where raging fire burned, and torment existed. But I wasn't simply listening to a story, it was as if

I was transported there as she was talking. I began to see hell in my mind's eyes. The experience was real, and I felt the never-ending torment of its reality.

I saw thousands upon thousands of prison cells lined up as high and as wide as I could see. I was in one of them. By myself. All alone. Freaked out. I knew others were in some of the other cells, but I couldn't see them. I saw the fire all around. Outside of the cell all I could see was bright orange and red fire that covered the ground, sky, and atmosphere. I couldn't see anything else. The fire seemed to be alive, reaching for me in my cell. I backed up against the wall trying to get away from it. I felt its torturous, painful burn but it wasn't consuming me. I didn't know how it wasn't killing me. I screamed. I wanted help and to get out, but I couldn't. I knew I would never be able to.

But the worst part of it all was the loneliness. The aching loneliness was a painful, deep void in my gut. And I somehow knew that God was up there somewhere, outside of that realm. I wanted to be with Him, but it wasn't possible. It was too late. I had deep regret. I could have known Him but I didn't. And there was nothing I could do. It was too late. And the pain of being all alone was terrible.

The experience was all the more real because it brought back a near-death experience I'd had when I was fifteen, while partying with friends in Daytona Beach. I mixed too many drugs together. I was told later at the hospital that I probably had a mild stroke, brought on by an extreme rise in body temperature. All I remember was feeling very strange and wanting and deciding to get out of the hot tub I was in. I stood up to walk away and as my body stiffened up like a board, I passed out and went backwards. Those who were nearby said it sounded like a bomb went off when my head hit the concrete below me. They rushed over to me, trying to get me to wake up, as I just laid there, lifeless.

I do not remember the fall, but I remember the experience while I was laying there. Everything was black. Pitch black. I could see nothing but darkness, and I'm not sure if I actually died or if I was in the process of dying. I felt as though I was being sucked into this vortex, this vacuum like a black hole that was automatically trying to pull me somewhere that I didn't want to go. I kept yelling, "*Mom! Don't let them take me! I can't go now! Mom! No! Don't let them take me*!" I did not say this out loud, so those around me couldn't hear it. But I could hear myself screaming.

And then, I woke up. I was having convulsions and saw the terrified people hovering over me and screaming at me to wake up. I was almost more frightened staring into their terrified faces, as I wasn't sure what was going on. They thought I died. I thought I died.

What I realized while listening to that tape in my car was that hell was indeed real and that I was going there that day when I was fifteen when I had that overdose.

Now at nineteen years old, I encountered the living God in my car through the testimony of that woman on the tape and my experiences with my personal *revelation of hell.*

I knew when I was listening to that tape that I was headed to hell, not only because of my sins, but because *I did not know God.* I sensed this giant God above me, and I felt so small under Him. I was *terrified.* I felt *so small.* I realized that He existed and I did *not* know Him and I *should* know Him. I was *terrified.* But that terror did not cause me to run away screaming. Within what seemed like half a second, I ran *to* God. Almost without thought, I ran to Him for safety, for salvation. I did not want to be separated from Him. My terror came from a sense of feeling separated from Him, and I knew I did not have to be. And faith helped me to believe in Him and run to Him.

It was like He appeared from out of nowhere. One minute I knew nothing of His existence and the next, He was right there, as if He was there all along and I never knew it. He was *much* bigger than me. I was no longer alone and that was very comforting…reassuring.

Another second after that, hope came into my mind and heart. I felt this freedom and felt like I could breathe. I said to myself, *I don't have to live like this* as I looked down at the drugs that were in my car. The addiction was broken and I threw my drugs out of the window.

Chapter Thirteen

The Book That Changed My Life

Sophia Asah

After my salvation experience, I checked into a twenty-eight-day rehab program and graduated. I had full intentions to quit everything for good. Although I'm sure the program advised me to, I made no plans to find a church, go to meetings, or surround myself with a good support group besides my close friend and college roommate. I had major blind spots. I appeared to do well in the rehab, but I underestimated how much I needed to change and what it was going to take. I felt removed from all the consequences and seemed to forget the pain rather quickly. I was back to my happy, fun, naïve self.

After a few months, I began to reason with myself that I could drink once a month. That idea lasted one month before it turned into once a week, then almost every day, even before my 8 a.m. college course. While I wasn't using drugs at that time, the addiction to alcohol came back with the same obsessive-compulsive behavior. The consequences weren't as severe, but I was just as miserable. It didn't take too long before I found the partiers who had access to drugs and had a major relapse.

I'll save you from the horror stories of the addictions, but deep within I was desperately looking for a way out. I didn't feel human. When I found out I had arrest warrants in three or four counties, I called the police department to turn myself in. They said it would take a few days for them to pick me up because the detective who was working on my case was out of town. *Can you believe that?* I waited a few days, a week maybe, I'm not sure, but they finally came and got me, and I felt so relieved. I wanted out. I wanted to be rescued, and I couldn't do it on my own.

At first, I faced a possible two months in jail. But then they asked me about this other county I was traveling in a few months back. Apparently, they caught me on camera committing a serious crime. I was now facing **fifteen years** in prison. It was no longer a short rescue mission where I could boast about my two-month "gangsta" time in the slammer. This was serious. But I now understand it was the best thing that could have happened.

It helped me to *surrender.*

I felt the most peace I had ever experienced. Not only because I was finally rescued from that awful lifestyle, but because Jesus Himself gave me peace. Along with that surrender came a desire to follow God wholeheartedly and to accept the consequences of what I had done. I took responsibility for my actions. I didn't blame other people or try to get out of it. I fully repented from *my way* and looked to Him to find *His way.*

I remember looking up, almost as if God was right there in front of me and said to Him, "*All I want is You, God. I don't care if I have to do fifteen years. I just don't want to go back to that way of life and all I want is You."* There was a supernatural love that God placed in my heart alongside a grace to trust in Him and surrender it all.

Somehow I knew that I needed to read the Bible. I felt I *had* to read it and sought out someone to help me know what to read. I met a woman who was awaiting a bus to take her to a federal prison, who told me to read Matthew, Mark, Luke, and John. I read those gospels and also flipped the Bible open and read whatever my eyes landed on. God spoke to me, without fail, no matter how or what I read in the Bible.

There were a few nights I couldn't sleep. The insomnia I had once experienced years before seemed to be coming back, and if you've ever had insomnia, you understand the feeling that you could go insane from the lack of sleep and the racing thoughts that run through your mind. I was determined not to go there again and decided to flip open the Bible for help. It landed right on Proverbs, "Do not be afraid, thy sleep shall be sweet." I needed specific help and my eyes landed right on the help I needed. I was shocked, stunned, in awe. My eyes opened wide, and I believed what I read. I trusted the words; I trusted God. And I slept like a baby that night.

This encounter brought me closer to trusting and believing in God and the Bible. I remember reading another passage shortly after that and thinking, *this book knows me.* It was way more than simply a book; it was the *Living* Word. I remember how the Bible knew secrets of my heart that I didn't even know. It unlocked the prison that not only my emotions and thoughts were in, but that I was in. Each word of truth somehow brought some freedom. His Word was so comforting, so reassuring. For the first time I didn't feel alone. I felt understood, guided, and known. I journaled and began to pray every day, every night, telling God *everything* that was on my heart. I held nothing back.

Chapter Fourteen

The Girl
Sophia Asah

I was extradited to another county three hours away, still facing the fifteen year sentence and awaiting a court date. After I arrived there, a new girl was placed into our cell pod. I saw her walk into the room like she was in slow motion. She walked in with a manly, confident strut, and I remember the instant attraction. I wanted her. We quickly became friends, and the attraction turned into our dating. For women to date other women in jail and prison is not only acceptable by the inmates, it can be esteemed. I had never seen such an encouragement to openly date another woman before this time. Their acceptance of us somehow removed the shame, as we didn't have to hide (except from the officers). It felt freeing. I felt comfortable in a relationship for the first time. And it was fun. We had a special companionship, and I truly believe we were both looking for love.

I was still reading the Bible. I loved God and had committed to following Him. Being with her didn't change that until I read something in the Bible.

I came across 1 Corinthians 6:9 where the Bible says that *homosexuals would not inherit the Kingdom of God*. I was by myself when I read those words, and as I put the book down, my eyes were opened wide. I may have said out loud, "It's a sin?!"

I was shocked. I had no idea it was wrong. I immediately ran to tell my girlfriend, "Hey did you know that what we are doing is a sin?" And she calmly responded that we were not in sin… because *we were in love*. She said the context of that verse was about lust and that wasn't the case with us.

No matter how much that could have made sense or how much I wanted to believe her, I couldn't because The Holy Spirit had already revealed the truth to me deep down in my heart. But, I wasn't ready to deal with that because I was already in love with her and I didn't want to have to deal with the conflict. I told her, "Okay" and pushed aside the truth.

At the time it was fun and the companionship was great. I was still being convicted by God, but I didn't think it was that big of a deal. It was one of those things that I put off like an over-due homework assignment. *I'll get to it later*. But the longer we spent time together, the more our bond grew. Likewise, the more time I spent with God, the more my bond grew with Him, too, and the conviction remained the same. Our lifestyle was a sin, and I needed to get out of it.

By the grace of God, my charges were reduced, and I only served six months in jail, with a one-year sentence in a residential rehab and five years of probation. I praise God for my mom who stood up in the courtroom, pleading with the judge to send me to rehab. I was relieved for multiple reasons. One was that I didn't have to go to prison, and the other that I would be physically removed from my girlfriend, ending our relationship, so I could follow God.

Internal Convictions

I mostly liked the rehab I was sentenced to and continued to follow God and read the Bible. My former cell-mate asked her mom to pick me up for church on Sundays and church became a source of encouragement to grow in my spiritual walk. Other than her mom and my new sponsor, it was totally up to me if I wanted to follow Jesus or not. I liked that no one made me, and I could cultivate this relationship on my own, without pressure or manipulation.

Not too much time passed when I found out my girlfriend would be coming to the same rehab. *What was I going to do*?! I was stressed, wondering how I was going to be able to hide the relationship from the counselors and still follow God.

I had already struggled with suicidal thoughts. But they increased during my struggle with homosexuality. The internal conflict was intense. I was attached to my girlfriend. Our mutual affection had grown quite serious and we talked about being together forever. And yet I was still getting convicted by the Lord. This internal battle caused so much stress.

At first, I didn't identify myself as a woman who was gay to stay. I didn't deny being in a gay relationship; it was more like I just *happened* to fall in love with a woman. But I began to realize that being gay was my identity. Like, that's who I was. The thought of giving it up was like asking someone to not be themselves. It felt like I would fall apart if I walked away from it. It was offensive to even consider changing who I was. It's not like asking someone to change their behavior. It is like asking someone to give up on themselves, and it's a terrifying feeling. So much so, that you want to protect and defend yourself at all cost.

My battle was not only an internal conflict, it was a *spiritual* battle. The struggle wasn't solely with my emotions and thoughts, nor was it just a struggle with society and conflict from people. There was a spiritual battle like what Ephesians 6 describes. I read that Satan came to "steal, kill, and destroy." I read that he is the "father of lies" and is the ultimate deceiver and accuser. It's not too hard to see why many people rationalize homosexuality and fight for human rights over biblical values. Satan was trying to lie to me about the truth in God's Word, but he was also tormenting me with fearful, anxious thoughts. He would tell me it's okay to be with her but then condemn me after I was with her. I felt like Father God was the one condemning me at times, putting a load of pressure on me, threatening me to straighten up or else. I now know that God is not condemning. He is full of grace and mercy. Satan is the accuser.

Holy Spirit convicted me, but He never condemned me. "There is no fear in love, but perfect love casts out fear" (1 John 4:18a NKJV). God wants us to follow Him because we love Him, not because we are afraid of being punished. When I read the Bible, He brought me to sweet scriptures from Psalm 139 where He told me how much He loved, me and from Jeremiah 29:11 where He told me He has good plans for me. But then I'd also read scriptures about wickedness and that what I was doing was *wicked*. The truth of those words felt like a log in my heart. My eyes would open wide up and the conviction seemed to stun me, put me in a place of accountability to *make a decision*. Every day that passed that I didn't *make a decision* to fully follow Christ seemed to weigh on me. A timer had been set, and I wouldn't have all the time in the world to decide. Time was running short. *Make a decision. Make a decision. Who are you going to follow?*

At first, the decision seemed like a choice between her and God. *Make a decision to be with her or to be with God*, but the more I worshipped Jesus, the less I worshipped myself. I discovered that my decision was not to follow her or God. Instead, it was a decision to follow *me or God.* What I wanted or what God wanted. *My* feelings, opinions and beliefs versus God's Word. The more I worshipped Jesus and kept choosing to seek Him every day, the more my life became about *Him* and what *He* wanted. *He died for me.* And now I wanted to choose to die as well. Die to what I wanted, die to my feelings, die to my desires, and live for Him. I believed the scripture that says, "If you lose your life for My sake, then you will find it" (Matthew 16:25).

"If you try to hang on to your life, you will lose it. But if you give up your life for my sake, you will save it" (Matthew 16:25 NLT).

Even now I can feel this strength well up from deep within my belly—power from the Holy Spirit to worship God and God alone. He is the only One worthy to live for.

Abba, Father, You are so good! Thank you for Your freedom! Thank you, Lord, for Your goodness! God, you never lie. In Your house is freedom and everlasting joy! You would never lead us into a destiny that wasn't the absolute Best. We trust You, God. We are not living for this life on this earth; there are eternal rewards in heaven for our obedience to You! Oh God, reveal Yourself to my friend reading this even now. I worship You. We worship You!

The Bible says,"Those who think they can do it on their own end up obsessed with measuring their own moral muscle but never get around to exercising it in real life. Those who trust God's action in them find that God's Spirit is in them—living and breathing God! Obsession with self in these matters is a dead end; attention to God leads us out into the open, into a spacious, free life. Focusing on the self is the opposite of focusing on God. Anyone completely absorbed in self ignores God, ends up thinking more about self than God. That person ignores who God is and what he is doing. And God isn't pleased at being ignored. But if God himself has taken up residence in your life, you can hardly be thinking more of yourself than of him" (Romans 8:5-9 THE MESSAGE).

In another translation, the God's Word, (GW) Translation, this same passage in Romans 8 says, "Those who live by the corrupt nature have the corrupt nature's attitude. But those who live by the spiritual nature have the spiritual nature's attitude. The corrupt nature's attitude leads to death. But the spiritual nature's attitude leads to life and peace. This is so because the corrupt nature has a hostile attitude toward God. It refuses to place itself under the authority of God's standards because it can't. Those who are under the control of the corrupt nature can't please God. But if God's Spirit lives in you, you are under the control of your spiritual nature, not your corrupt nature" Whoever doesn't have the Spirit of Christ doesn't belong to him (GW).

I had a strong desire to live for Him, but the journey was not over. It would be another two years before my relationship with her was finally over. I continued to battle between my decision to follow Him or follow myself. And God continued to love me unconditionally and strengthen me in His Word. I learned how to let the Word of God be a sword that fought off the demons that were tormenting me and causing me to remain stuck in lies and in bondage.

He could have done it all at once. God could have saved me from the battle, but He had greater plans. Psalm18:34 says that He "trains our hands for battle." He is not in a panic or freaked out because of our sin. He wants our willing hearts to love Him back and to understand our royal position as children of God. We have been given authority over sin and Satan, and nothing has to prevail over us. His intentions are not just to do everything *for us,* but to partner *with us*, empowering us to overcome and rise up as men and women of faith. And that is exactly what happened. I learned to wrestle with my flesh and with demons until the truth prevailed, and I got set free. I had a lot of help along the way and will share that with you in the following chapters.

Chapter Fifteen

The Journey and Pivotal Moments
Sophia Asah

In an attempt to get more strength to walk out of that relationship (and to test their courage), I approached several believers and asked them if they thought homosexuality was a sin. Part of the reason I asked was because I needed help following God's will, and I thought if they agreed with the Word, it would help strengthen my ability to follow God. I was also testing them. I put them on the spot and perhaps was a little intimidating. Most of them, just as I suspected, looked at me with fear and backed down. It seemed that they didn't want to hurt my feelings or invoke any more conflict and slowly sputtered out words like, "It's not up to me to judge" and "that's between you and God" and "love covers sin so it only matters that you love."

On the inside I was harsh towards them, "You cowards. Can't even speak the truth. Weak Christians. You clearly aren't sold out to Jesus." On the outside I smiled at them, and took their *kind* words to encourage me to stay in the sin.

During that time, I needed someone to lovingly tell me the truth. "Yes, this is a sin." I was searching for what God's Word said because I wanted to follow Jesus. (At the same time, there can be a wisdom in not just telling someone that they are in sin. Having an eagerness to call out sin *can* be immature. Knowing how to respond or what to say really requires wisdom.)

My Sponsor

I chose a woman who was involved in Bible studies in jail, to be my sponsor. I asked her to sponsor me when I got into the rehab. She was a former drug addict and was known to be straight-forward and tough. I chose her because I wanted something real. I didn't want fluff. And I knew she had the guts to not hold back and to speak the truth. I know me and my ability to charm my way in and out of situations and manipulate people. I did not want to do that. I needed someone to cut through my crap and see me beyond the walls I put up.

I called her every day and worked through "The Twelve Steps" with her. Because I hadn't been struggling with the drug and alcohol addiction anymore, most of the focus was on the relationship with my girlfriend. She supported me and continually held me accountable to the conviction of my sin. She taught me to look at *my part* in every situation, which was really tough. I realized how much I blamed people and played the victim game. She was instrumental in pointing me in the direction of taking responsibility for my emotions and choices.

Taking responsibility is something that I could not do on my own, no matter how powerful my prayer life and God's Word. I needed support. I trusted her and let her into my life. I confessed my lies, my mistakes, and more importantly, learned to be honest about my motives and about my secret plans *before* I executed them. It was so challenging to tell on myself and not pretend to be this perfect person; it was freeing. I learned not to try and figure things out on my own or rely on myself to overcome my issues. I could rely on God and her. I trusted her. In fact, I would feel stressed and even in bondage *until* I confessed my motives and sin. Confess your sins to one another so that you may be healed (James 5:16a and c ESV). The moment I chose to not hide in the dark and expose my junk, the light came in and set me free.

Kicked out of Church

When I was in jail, my Bunkie told her mom, Mary, that I would be going to the rehab near her house. When I got out, Mary came to pick me up every Sunday for church. Mary brought me to a great church where the preacher really knew how to break down the Bible line by line. There was a biblical counselor that I had begun meeting with to help me walk away from the gay lifestyle. She talked a lot about putting off your old self and putting on your new nature in Christ (Ephesians 4:22-24). It made sense but it seemed really hard to just *do that.*

There was a Bible study group that I joined consisting mostly of older women. I didn't really get to know them that well, but it was nice to be there. After several months of attending, the pastor's wife (who led the Bible study) privately came to me and read 1 Corinthians 5:11. She simply read the verse to me and said, "*What am I supposed to do with this?*" She was in a predicament. That scripture says that "*if a believer in your midst continues in sin, you are not to hang around them. Instead, remove them from your midst."* Her goal was for my repentance and a return to my senses.

(For reference, 1 Corinthians 5:11 GW: Now, what I meant was that you should not associate with people who call themselves brothers or sisters in the Christian faith but live in sexual sin, are greedy, worship false gods, use abusive language, get drunk, or are dishonest. Don't eat with such people.)

I was stumped. Yea, what *is* she supposed to do with that verse? You can't just ignore it or keep the parts that you like. While I was offended at first, the offense didn't last because my sponsor had told me to look at *my part* and to be responsible for my reactions in every situation. This understanding helped me to see what God wanted to say to me and not just be angry at the pastor's wife.

Because I really did want to walk with Jesus in love and truth, I was able to hear Him clearly. My dilemma wasn't about the preacher's wife. The only thing that was staring at me in the face was the reality that I had a decision to make, would I choose God or my selfish desires? And I was scared.

I was scared because I couldn't (or wouldn't) wholeheartedly commit to end the relationship but I knew I needed to be in a good church. I didn't have another conversation with the preacher's wife to work through it. I didn't like conflict and to me, the door seemed to shut on that church because she kicked me out (but actually, I wasn't fully ready to walk out of the sin). So, I prayed about it and decided to choose to attend the church that my sponsor was going to.

Meeting with the new Pastor

I believe God gave my new pastor wisdom when I called him to ask to meet with my girlfriend and me. I desperately wanted him to tell her that what we were doing was a sin so that she would also follow God and make it easier for me to end the relationship for good. But, he took a different approach. He simply stated "because of our different views about the Scripture, our relationship just wouldn't ever be able to work out for us." His words were wisdom. Sure, he could have taken the opportunity to call out the sin and tell her she was wrong and be on my side. But she wasn't even in a place where she was searching for truth or open to it. And although I was desperate to follow God, I wasn't thinking of what would help her. I just wanted the pastor to tell her that the Bible said it was a sin and she was wrong. In my mind, that would have worked and she would now be faced with the truth of what I already knew. It made logical sense. But I believe the wrong spirit was trying to operate in me on that day and the pastor made a wise decision.

In my opinion, when someone isn't interested in following Jesus, the main issue is not their sin, but the person's *unbelief* in who Jesus is and what He has done for them. For me, I was interested in following Jesus, but the stronghold of the sin tried to pull me into unbelief of God's Word (even though He had clearly convicted me of it over and over). Hebrews 3:19 says that they "could not enter into rest because of their unbelief."

When it comes to having conversations about homosexuality, we really need to listen to God and to the person or people with whom we are speaking. Immaturity can cause us to be hasty or pridefully spout all that we know, and we can end up sounding like a "clanging gong or a noisy symbol" (1 Corinthians 13:1). Maturity waits patiently to hand out the pearls. We need to think of relationship and ask God to draw people's hearta to Him, not just lay down the law. But we also need to be courageous and speak truth, because the truth sets people free. It can be tough to know what to say in every situation, but I believe Holy Spirit will give us wisdom when we need it.

NA Meetings

The rehab required us to attend twelve-step meetings. I chose NA (Narcotics Anonymous) because I could relate more to the drug addicts, and it was a younger community. Those meetings were a blessing, and the twelve steps are an incredible way to grow for any person, drug addict or not.

NA upheld a lot of biblical principles, like confessing your sins. The meetings encouraged us to share our darkest secrets without shame or condemnation. The people went out of their way to pick up an addict for a meeting or answer the phone at two a.m. for someone who was struggling. We learned a sense of community and doing life together. The people were fun and didn't have as many walls up as you might find in some church settings.

There was an acceptance for wherever you were at on your journey without pressure to change in order to be liked or loved. Part of that was because people were dying all the time and the only goal was to get clean and sober. If you were alive and sober another day, it truly was a miracle.

On the other hand, they did not follow all biblical principles. In the culture of my NA group in our area, homosexuality was not only accepted, but esteemed. This made it easy to be with my girlfriend. They embraced us, just as the jail embraced us, and I found a way to ignore my conscience and God when I was there. I could be with my girlfriend without the conviction (until I got home later that night or when it hit me in the early morning).

Bible Study: Round Two

I joined another Bible study at this new church with women my own age. While I went there to get help walking out of the gay lifestyle, I didn't really want them *too* involved with my life. I guess I thought that if I got strengthened enough in the Lord by hanging around people who viewed homosexuality as a sin, then that part of my life would just quietly disappear, and I wouldn't have to deal with their reaction to me. But, as we got into conversation, everyone was sharing their heart and it seemed like an appropriate time and place to let them know about me too.

I remember feeling relieved, and it didn't seem like I shocked anyone. It was almost like sharing what color socks I had on."*Oh, that's nice Sophia." So glad you're here. Nice to meet you.* Of course, another friend of mine who was in that same Bible study said she looked around the room and saw how much they were judging me so she decided not to share that she had a boyfriend that just got out of prison and who she was sleeping with. Now, I don't know if her past experiences of judgmental Christians gave her the wrong perspective or if they really were judgmental. But either way, I didn't care at that point; I just wanted to be free.

A New Culture

Would you believe that most of those girls in that Bible study (we were in our mid to upper twenty's and even thirty's) were virgins? Talk about a drastically different culture! The concept of purity was new to me, but I craved it. I craved holiness and cleanliness. I had felt so dirty and wanted to be clean.

I was amazed that most of them had been following God since they were children and decided to remain pure until marriage. That seemed crazy. I came from a drug addicted lifestyle where sex of any and every kind with any person was the norm. *So, to be around virgins?* I loved it, to be honest. There was so much innocence. I wanted that. I could feel God restoring me to my innocence just by hanging around them.

During one of our Bible studies, they allowed my mom to attend since she was in town visiting me for a few days. During that particular Bible study, the young man next door knocked on the door and came in. He wanted to make some kind of announcement, so we all just looked at him and waited for him to tell us. I still remember that moment when he said, "I wanted to let you all know that I asked Terra if I could date her and she said yes. We are courting."

My jaw lowered and my mouth hung wide open. I looked around the room. Some of the girls already knew he was going to come over and said, "Yay! We are so happy for you guys," as they cheered them on. I was still like, *what in the world is happening?* It was cool but also so foreign. *Who does that*? My mom thought the same thing, that it was really sweet and something she had never seen before.

Now, I'm not saying there is any standard way to announce your dating or courting someone, but I felt a sense of honor. Innocence. Purity. Courage. Intentionality. They were courting with the intentions of pursuing marriage, not just enjoying a fling or hooking up secretly. There was no shame. They were living in the light, the light of Christ, and wanted the support and accountability of their friends. They didn't want to hide and they wanted to go about this process with Jesus in their midst. They were living for God in their relationship and I had never seen, or heard, anything like it. They were doing life God's way, to the best they knew how, and that was exactly what I too wanted.

Roommate

I am grateful for a former roommate who was going through a nasty divorce and invited me to rent a room in her million-dollar home.

I was *still* battling homosexuality. One day, I was screaming in emotional agony, curled up into a ball on the floor of the kitchen, when she walked in. She couldn't stand seeing me that way and yelled, "I don't care what you choose! I will love you whatever you decide! I just don't want to see you going on this way!" It was exactly what I needed to hear in that moment. Unconditional love. I felt the love of God through her words. That completely melted and softened my heart to the point that I stopped crying, the mental anguish ceased, and I felt peace knowing that I could choose to be with my girlfriend or not and God will love me the same.

All the pressure to choose this or that went away. You cannot possibly make a good choice when you're being forced to or are feeling a ton of pressure. God died to set us free from the "have-to's." He simply says, "Follow Me…if you want to." And if we don't, it will suck for us and we won't have a blessed life, but He still loves us. His love doesn't change. In that moment, when I felt the freedom to choose either way, my real desire came to the surface.

I wanted out of homosexuality. I wanted God.

First Mission Trip

I went on a mission trip to South America. I remember sitting on top of a mountain, grieved that I was still with my girlfriend (Isn't God so patient?). I thought, *Okay, it is official.*

I am on a mission trip. This officially makes me a Christian, and I just cannot be dating a woman. Shortly after that trip, I broke up with her for the last time.

The breakup felt like a great idea until five or six81 days went by when I missed her and wanted her back again. But this time, she had already found a new girlfriend. I was so hurt. *How can she forget about me that easily?* (I feel badly for her now. All that I put her through. She kept staying with me up until then, but I really put her through a ringer.)

I told my Bible study teacher what happened and that's when she confessed her silent prayer. My Bible study teacher silently prayed that the next time my girlfriend and I broke up, that my girlfriend would find someone else to date immediately so we couldn't get back together. Sure enough, the last time we broke up, she started dating someone that same week. And I knew. I knew God was doing for me what I could not do for myself. I would never get back with her – or any other girl ever again.

Chapter Sixteen

Healing
Sophia Asah

Healing After the Storm

When I broke up with my girlfriend, I didn't struggle too much with same sex attraction or have a strong desire to date another woman. What I *did* struggle with was the thought of dating a man (and truly understanding/embracing my feminine nature). I had no attraction to men. In fact, I hated men, and I was afraid of them. They were an unknown species to me. But God seemed to be saying to me, *Be abstinent. I'm not asking you to date a man. Just stay abstinent.* I was willing to be single for the rest of my life if it meant walking with God wholeheartedly. It was scary, but I was willing.

There was a man my age who also attended the NA meetings. He asked me to hang out a few times. He was good looking and sweet. He never tried to have sex with me, which was very different for me. We simply had fun together. After a few months of hanging with him I remember thinking, *Well, maybe I could someday date a guy.* That was certainly a seed of possibility.

Hearing from God and the Anointing

I continued to follow God and began learning about inner healing in my church. This ministry was more than counseling—it was Holy Spirit led prayer, facilitated by a trained person, that got to the roots of issues. What may take *ten years* in counseling may take *two hours* in an inner healing session!

I also grew in the prophetic gifts and learned how to hear from God in greater levels, which gave me direction and guidance for every area of my life, personally and professionally.

I learned how to hear from God while I was in jail, simply by reading the Word, praying, and journaling. It is simple. Stay in the Word, spend some time with Him, and ask Him to speak to you through pictures in your mind, a song, thoughts, words, signs, journaling, etc.

I sensed Him asking me to spend time with Him in my room twice a week. *And do what?*

I sensed His sweet calling, *Just spend time with Me.*

I committed to spending time with Him and for the next several years, went into my room every Monday and Wednesday night for at least two hours and learned how to wait on His Holy Spirit to direct me into worship, prayer, or reading the Bible. I remember that a certain church was going through some kind of awakening, and they would live-stream their services. People were sharing their testimonies of how God would heal them physically, emotionally and mentally. As I listened, faith rose in me for the same things for myself and others. I got to pray for others for healing and I myself found healing from anxiety and fears and such. I learned how to take up the authority that Christ gave me and how to discern the schemes of the enemy and partner with others to tear down works of darkness in prayer. It was during this time that I would "tarry in my room until He clothed me with power from on high," Luke 24:49. From that secret prayer place, His anointing fell stronger upon me. One particular area in which this anointing was useful, was the local rehab and county jail. His anointing was on me to heal and set the captives free through preaching and praying for them.

The third church I found had a strong prophetic worshipping community. They brought me into the presence of God, and there was a synergy and a unique dynamic when we came together. In the Holy Spirit, we ministered to one another and went away full and satisfied. Prayer in my own home was great, but it was on a higher level with other believers. I sat in worship with them for hours at a time, encountering Jesus. We also prayed for each other as Holy Spirit led us to. I had visions of heaven and journaled what He spoke to my heart.

I even went to the youth group there when I was twenty-five! I thought it was interesting that God met me, a twenty-five year old woman, at a youth group where teenagers were able to show me love and teach me about gifts because they were so mature in the Lord and understood their identity and belonging in Christ as well as operate in the gifts of Prophecy and Healing. I remember sitting on the floor bawling my eyes out and being ministered to and comforted by a teen. I cried all the time in God's presence. I couldn't figure out why, but I think He was healing my heart. He spoke to my heart. And how precious that I was being ministered to by the teenagers. I was just so hungry for God. And so broken. But God was healing me!

Healing with Men and Authority

One day, I was in my house, sitting on my couch, and God took me through a personal little inner healing session. God brought me back to that place when I was a teenager, when my dad was walking out on my mom and me. I saw a picture of myself holding up a sign that said, "I DON'T NEED MEN." That sign and declaration was still lodged in my heart. For a long while, it served to protect me. But now, God was asking me to tear down that sign. I didn't want to. But He had humbled me. I was so angry at all the men that hurt me through neglect, rape, misuse, and rejection. But, I was the one who ended up repenting. I had also treated them with less than respect and made poor choices. For a long time, it was hard to see what *I* did through the pain of what *they* did. But when you're wrestling with God, the truth will prevail if you don't give up. And His truth will set you free.

I began to reason with myself. *It's ridiculous to think that I don't need half of the human race. Half of the population. I just don't need men?! Come on Sophia. You can't just cut half the human race out of your life.* And then, I was finally willing to tear that sign down. I declared aloud, I *NEED MEN!* And as I made that declaration, that sign came crumbling down, and God healed yet another layer of my heart. That sign, that declaration, that stronghold would have never allowed me to be married to a man. It would have never allowed me to be in *any* healthy relationship with a man, whether business or personal.

A few years later, God brought some more healing to my heart. I was working more closely with my pastor in ministry, and it was obvious that I had some issues with authority. Frankly, I didn't trust anyone in authority: the government, my parents, grandparents, church leaders, teachers, pretty much everyone in authority, *especially* men.

I had grown up with a good father, but he didn't communicate his heart much. I didn't know what was going on inside of him and, by default, it made me suspicious of men. Then due to all the damage from the sexual immorality and rapes, and never gaining an opportunity to grow really close to men, I hadn't been able to bridge that gap yet. I had great examples of men in the church, but I didn't get very close to most of them. I kept a wall up, I'm sure. But some of them just sort of backed away. Like, "Don't get too close to me. You're not safe." Even the married ones would kind of hide behind their wives. Maybe I had a spirit of seduction still on me that made them nervous. I don't know, but my point is, I hadn't developed trust or a real connection with men.

Our new pastor's wife encouraged him to communicate with his sheep and be in relationship with us. There was an open door to grow together. One day, I called him up to have a meeting with him. I had been at his church for several years and struggled with resentments against him. I could not seem to get rid of them no matter how hard I tried to forgive and rebuke the devil. I just kept getting mad and feeling hurt. He agreed to the meeting and brought his wife.

I felt that I needed to be honest. If I was ever going to be healed, I needed to work through this crap. So, at the meeting, I proceeded to lay out all the things that he did that made me mad. At one point I think I even told him that I struggled with thoughts of hating him. God really gave him grace because he responded with love and wisdom.

He went through each item I had said and was honest. His response was either, "You are right. I should not have done that and I am sorry." Or, "I wish you would have asked me to explain why I was doing that. You are misunderstanding my heart and that's not at all what I meant or what happened." I wanted the truth and he was being truthful.

That meeting built a new level of trust and a new ability to be honest and communicate, not only with men, but women too. I hadn't grown up in a house where I felt safe enough to be vulnerable, or question what the other person was doing, or let others question what I was doing. There was no discussion. There was dictatorship from one and avoidance from the other. As a result, I learned to do both. I was both a dictator *and* I avoided, depending on what was easier or seemed to help me in each situation. And I was stressed. That conversation was yet one of the many ways in which I learned how to better communicate.

Healing with my Husband

God brought my husband and me together after I had been single for ten years. The first half of those years I was a free bird and the thought of being in a relationship freaked me out, so I didn't mind the singleness. The second half, I felt ready and cried out for God to bring me a husband. There were many times of deep, aching loneliness. All I knew was to desperately draw closer to God and almost every time I did, I found satisfaction in Christ. He filled my heart with His love and I often felt a profound sense of relief knowing that it was Jesus that I really wanted. Had I given in to my desire for a man and chased after my feelings, I would have only been trying to satisfy the deeper longing for deep fellowship with God.

I met my husband through a mutual friend. I would have never guessed that he was "it" but I do remember looking into his eyes and feeling safe because it didn't seem like he was hiding anything. There was a purity in his eyes and I felt like he could be a friend. And he was. For about nine months before we started dating. It's a beautiful story, and I am so blessed to have waited on God for the best He had for me: he was worth the wait.

We built a solid foundation while we were dating. I had prayed, "God, I want a solid foundation. I don't want to be married twenty years and just begin to deal with things that should have been dealt with in the beginning." My parents got divorced after being married for more than twenty years and I did not want divorce, so I was intentional about facing whatever came up, and it was messy at times.

The challenges that arose weren't solely because I had come from a homosexual background. By that time, I had already been healed from most of the hatred and fear that I harbored against men. I think a lot of challenges arose because I had no clue about the male species and was still learning how to communicate. And, yea, I think I still had trust issues with men.

We fell into a pattern similar to my parents (and other couples) where the man avoided or withdrew and the woman attacked or demanded conversations. Plus, we both had anger issues and were easily triggered by one another's reactions. This pattern drove me almost insane. The worst part was how much the devil would roam around our midst, causing the intensity to increase to what was almost unbearable for me.

A few times, I cried out to God, *Why did you make men and women so different*? I was mad at God for making it so difficult to communicate with him. It was so much easier to talk to a woman. Not so with this man. We absolutely misunderstood each other, got frustrated, attacked and wouldn't listen. I felt that I was constantly in a spiritual battle, trying to discern what was going on and it was just so much easier to talk with other women.

But God was faithful and we both began to grow. Every time I thought that he didn't care, he was actually thinking through things and didn't know what to say or how to say it. And every time he thought I was bringing something up to start a fight, he learned to express his emotions and let me in.

We learned to set aside time for family meetings where we could bring up issues that were on our heart in a safe place. I was almost always the one to start, but that would open a door for him to express himself too.

We learned to call out the devil when we sensed something wasn't right. We would say aloud, "Hey, I'm feeling something." Then, we would come together and tell the devil to leave. Satan always leaves when you chase him away in the name of Jesus. The atmosphere would immediately shift, and we were able to work through our conflict. The friction was ridiculous until we took authority.

I am so grateful we made it through that trying time because the gift of being married to him is the best! God blessed our union. We waited until marriage to be intimate and I must tell you, there is nothing better than having a marriage that is blessed by our heavenly Father! And now we are having a child!

There is so much opportunity to grow in marriage. It's really amazing. It's the fire that brings our impurities, insecurities, fears, anger, and junk to the surface. We can blame the other person or we can ask God what our part is and work on our own junk first. When both people are seeking the Lord and are willing to grow, change can happen more quickly. Breakthroughs are a regular part of our life and although we aren't always on the same page at the same time, it doesn't take too long for God to get us on the same page. Today, my hubby and I are best friends. We laugh all the time, and I have more fun with him than any person on the planet. We love to work together, make up random songs to sing, eat healthy, exercise, travel, and do life together. I am constantly in awe at how much love is in our midst.

Being married to a man is one of the most beautiful gifts God has given me. There is a sense of completion and fulfillment, a healthy challenge that gives opportunity to grow into your potential. I love his masculinity and how it complements and even brings out my true feminine nature. I love how my femininity makes room for his God given masculine nature to be fulfilled. There were many moments that he would say something that healed deep places in my heart, healing that could only come through a man. I am learning how to love and respect him more and more every day. My heart has grown tender and compassionate towards men. They are often misunderstood. But, like us women, they have fears and insecurities that can manifest in odd ways. It's important to take the time to understand what is going on behind the surface. Men are amazing, strong creatures.

Being Re-Parented

I watched a DVD series on parenting and raising children. Since my husband and I are about to have our first child, we know we need as much help as we can get. As the speaker talked about areas of discipline, I was thinking, O*h man. I need help in those areas. How am I going to help my kids when I'm weak in those areas?*

The speaker continued saying that if we are weak in certain areas of relationships, finances, work ethics, it could be that we were never trained up in those areas as a child. Maybe your parents didn't know how to teach certain things to you so you never actually learned…but somehow as an adult, as if by magic, we are supposed to know how to do certain things?

As I watched that DVD series, I sensed my heavenly Father in the room with me. He reminded me that it's okay that I'm weak and immature in certain areas. I can be trained in them, and He wants to raise me up as His daughter. I am and will always and forever be living in my Father's house. I know God as a loving Father. I didn't always know Him to be this way, but I do now. A perfect, gentle, respectful, protective, nurturing, caring, warrior who looks out for my best and has a ton of grace for me to learn and grow. Just as we will be raising our child soon, we can allow our Abba Father to raise us.

Not having the proper training leaves us with dysfunctions and voids. The good news is that we can bring that to God and allow Him to re-parent us.

I have had many experiences where God took me back to my childhood and healed memories. He showed up, as pictures in my mind, and redeemed the memory. He is so faithful to give us new memories that replace the old ones that still cause us pain. We don't have to remain broken due to wounds and sin. A good friend of mine is writing a book about being twice broken.[30] God will use painful things and allow us to be broken. This brokenness can lead us to surrender, salvation, and humility before God. It can lead us to a wonderful relationship with Him and healing and righteousness. The second brokenness is the one we choose to walk in. It occurs not because of bad things that happen, but because of our willingness to remain moldable, tender, surrendered children in His loving care.

Chapter Seventeen

Go Into All The World

Sophia Asah

A few years back, I went through a rigorous leadership training program with my husband. It was a step of faith for me because the program was secular and had a reputation for having some new age techniques and attracting a strong LGBTQ community. I was afraid to enter into such an environment because I only want to be influenced by the Holy Spirit, but at this point, I knew that I could trust my husband and that God was leading him.

I was right. The environment was a mixture of Christians and atheists, biblical truths and demonic teachings. And I was also right in the sense that God had truly led us there to learn some things that we weren't learning inside of the church.

I can remember they had us go through a trust exercise in which it was revealed that I didn't easily trust most people, especially unbelievers. Suspicion holds people at a distance and guarded people find it very difficult to truly connect with others. While I am a social person and genuinely enjoy being around most people, I had many walls up between me and unbelievers. It took that exercise to reveal the truth of where I really stood regarding people who didn't know Jesus. It was the first time since I had been saved that I was in an environment where I was pushed past my comfort zone to open my heart, drop my fears and pride, and get to know the others in the group.

Unknowingly, I had been hiding in the church bubble to protect myself from "those" people and from outside dangers. I felt as though they (and the demons on them) could harm me with their ungodly influence. I had become the opposite of what Jesus has called us to be: *lights in the world.* He never called us to become lights within the church or commission us to "go into all the safe rooms in your house and local churches and preach the gospel and heal the broken hearted." He told us to go into the "world," which means the secular environments where Jesus is not currently dwelling. He told us He was "sending us out as sheep among wolves" and to be "harmless as a dove and wise as a serpent" (Matthew 10:16). And He gave us His Holy Spirit to show us how to do this and gifted us with gifts and an anointing that can help others to get set free and come to know Christ as Savior.

This wasn't exactly new for me, and yet it was. I was working and volunteering in secular environments and regularly shared Jesus and asked to pray for people, but I was coming from a place of "you need me" and the interactions felt more like an outreach project than relationship. I ministered and prayed and really did care for them, but I also wasn't going to go out of my way to develop friendships with them. I wanted them to come to where *I* was, but was unwilling (scared and ignorant) to meet them where *they* were.

Conversation with my transgender Friend

Some of the purpose of the secular training was to discover your dreams and make a difference in the world. One of the women was transgender and had her surgery scheduled. She had been living as a man for several years and mostly was able to pass as a man. She was one of the most kind-hearted, loving people I have ever met.

In order to pursue her dreams of promoting education about transgenderism, she opened up a group discussion where she would share and ask anyone if they had questions. I mostly listened and then asked if I could have a one on one follow up with her.

She graciously agreed and we set up our time to chat. She mostly knew where I stood in terms of that subject, but she took the risk to have a conversation with me. I was a little nervous but I also felt the freedom to be vulnerable as she wasn't the type of person who got angry and attacked. Anyway, I asked her all kinds of questions about her childhood and what her relationship was like with her dad. What things had been like for her, etc. And then she asked me questions.

I told her my story: The horrors of the addiction and my relationship with the girl. And how I was convicted that it was a sin when I read it in the bible. I told her that Jesus' love was greater than anything I had found on this earth and though the struggle was tough and I didn't understand at times, I truly wanted Him over her or my own life. I then asked her if she knew Jesus. She grew up in a traditional denomination. I'm not sure if she actually ever had a relationship with Him or not.

I then told her that I was afraid to share with her my convictions on homosexuality and transgenderism being a sin, because I didn't want to be labeled as a hateful Christian. I didn't want my heart to be misunderstood. I told her that I rarely ever talk about the subject because it is so sensitive and I don't want to be put into that category of hateful Christians. I asked her, "Do you think that I hate you because I view this as sin?"

And she simply said, "No. Not at all. Those are your views and you are allowed to have them." I felt relieved. And accepted by her. She asked me if I wanted to help convert gay people into becoming straight. She began to recommend organizations that help people who want to become straight. I was blown away! But then I told her, "Well, I am not really looking to convert anyone. I just want to share my story, introduce people to Jesus, and offer another option for them if they want to get out of the LGBTQ lifestyle."

That is still how I feel. I'd like to share my story, let people know how wonderful Jesus is and that He died to save us from our sins, and offer another option. Many people don't know of the healing power of Jesus and are being convinced that there is no other way other than to go with what "feels right." What feels right may be a lie.

The last thing we talked about during that conversation was the Bible. She said it was *subject for interpretation.* Meaning, it could be interpreted in more than one way. She didn't believe there was only one way to interpret it and she also didn't believe it held a final truth. In fact she thought that she was responsible for coming up with her own truth and living by that standard that she has set. This was where we could not agree because I believe that God has a standard that He sets in His Word for us. My motivation is not to try and discover what makes sense to me, but what God is saying in His Word.

That is where we could not come to agreement. It came down to the truth found in God's Word, and she simply did not hold that as her standard. Ah. You see, when I read The Bible, I was convicted that if God said it was sin, then it was sin and I needed to conform to His standard, trusting that it was the best for me. She interpreted the Bible in her own way and didn't hold the Bible to be true and had essentially become her own god, making up her own rules, according to her standard, according to the enormous amount of research she had done. She did not serve God. She served the philosophy of the world.But I know there are people who are being convicted by Holy Spirit to surrender their lives. People, just like me, who are recognizing the deception that has held them captive to do the devil's will. People, just like me, who have an inner desire to want to know God and a pull to discover what is true. This is why we are writing this book, to help those who are on their journey of discovering what God says is true and being set free by it.

Friendly Neighbors

Around that same time, my husband and I got to know some of the people in his neighborhood. The next-door neighbors, who weren't going to church at all, treated me with such kindness and love and went out of their way to help me with the yard on many occasions, even mulching our flowerbeds with his leftover mulch while we were on a work trip! They also invited us over for dinner frequently. The man was a grill master. He had four grills (one was a smoker) and would smoke cheese or some kind of meat for eighteen hours. The aroma was enticing and he almost always saved us a dish even if we couldn't make dinner. You can't get any better neighbors than that! I was in a vulnerable place because I didn't know anyone else and honestly needed some friends. Had I been "too busy" to need their friendship, I might not have appreciated their kindness. It was the kind of normal that I had been missing. This couple showed me how to be a "normal" Christian and cultivate simple friendships around me. I could still have a fire in my bones and go on mission trips, but I could also do the work of the Lord right in my back yard where it's not as glamorous but oh so sweet and precious…and desperately needed in our independent culture.

Chapter Eighteen

Sophia's Interview With Linda
Linda's Story

Linda struggled with trans*gender* desires and has since been trans*formed.* This is an account of how I met her and my recent interview of her.

I met Linda on an airplane coming back from a mission trip to the Philippines. I overheard her telling her story and turned around to ask if I could hear more. We exchanged numbers but didn't have time to talk because we were de-boarding the plane. I realized she lived close to where I lived (of all things!) and we scheduled a meeting at the Indianapolis airport.

I was a little nervous, as I hadn't been around many transgender or ex-transgenders before that point. Although I tried to think of her as how God created her, I wondered if she would seem more like a man or woman when I sat down to talk with her. As soon as I met her, she seemed like a woman. Had I not known her story, I would have never guessed she struggled with this issue. From the moment I looked into her eyes and she opened her mouth, I could tell she was free. Like totally free. Freer than most people, *than most Christians*, I had met.

Her story and the anointing on her life is evident. She is a wonderful, brilliant leader and I hope you are encouraged by her story.

Sophia: "What actions and words of people drew you to want to *know* Jesus? What actions and words of Christians *repelled* you?"

Linda: "Nobody knew what I was struggling with until I told my campus pastor at age twenty-one. I was in church but didn't say anything because no one was really talking about that sort of thing in the church (this was in the late 1980's/early 90's) or if they were talking about it, it was all negative. I was too terrified to say anything in fear of them shaming me or treating me like some sort of monster.

In 1991 I kneeled down privately before the Lord and told him that I wanted to be a man and was attracted to women, and asked Him to take it away (she had hoped He would and it would all go away and she wouldn't have to tell anyone).

It didn't just go away.

In 1994 I went to a conference and heard a speaker talk about how to get free from habitual sin. I knew I'd never get set free until I told someone. I was terrified but desperate to be free.

My campus pastor had no idea. (Linda was a part of church leadership at the time.) I decided to tell him and braced myself inwardly. I was expecting reproof but instead, he said, "*We love you and this doesn't change our opinion of you. We see the calling on your life and want you to get the help that you need.*"

I heard Holy Spirit say, "*I feel the same and I am sad for you. I want you to get help.*"

I had such a skewed view of God and thought for sure that He hated me and was mad at me. (Linda said that God showed His true loving nature through her pastor's words which restored her view of God.)"

Sophia: "What was your healing process like?"

Linda: (She laughs with a small sigh.) "Eleven years. It was an eleven-year process. My pastor said this was outside of his area and connected me with an Exodus Counselor to get professional help. The counselor was a man who had come out of homosexuality. (She met with him a few times and he thought at first he could help her since he could relate, but realized she needed to connect with another female Christian counselor.) When I met with the new counselor, I (didn't want to but knew I had to) talked about how I wanted male genitalia. When I told her, she kind of laughed it off and seemed to not take me seriously.

I was disappointed that it was taking so long to change.

In 1996 I went to a Pentecostal Church (Linda had a Presbyterian background). The woman who was preaching was following the leading of the Holy Spirit and came off stage and said to me, "*The Lord wants you to know that He wanted you to be a little girl.*" There was no way she could have known anything about me, but Holy Spirit let her know. I knew in that moment that I was not hidden from God (in a good way).

I grew up in a campus crusade type of ministry and women didn't teach and preach. I thought that desire was the transgender stuff coming up so I died to the call of God on my life.

The Pentecostal preacher then told me that I was "*called to preach and teach.*" (Again, this woman was speaking specific things to her that no one but God could have known and it restored her calling.)

She also said, "*There is coming a day when you will look in the mirror and think, 'I like me, I don't hate me.*'" I didn't know how that was going to happen, but my spirit said, "Yes! I just kept seeking Jesus and held on to the hem of His garment."

Sophia: "Did you tell anyone else after that or keep it to yourself?"

Linda: "I became honest and told other people my struggles and found great freedom… but they didn't know what to do with me.

Then I realized that I was very attracted to my pastor's wife who I was in ministry with. (Linda planned to quit the leadership team because of it and decided to confess to her what was going on in her heart.) The pastor's wife looked at me and told me that she was deeply attracted to her husband alone and they came to me and said, '*We are going to love you through this. You were broken in relationships and God is going to heal you through relationships.*' She ended up becoming a spiritual mother to me.

Then for the first time I met someone who had also dealt with transgender desires. (Linda said she felt understood and not alone; it was relieving.) That's when he told me about inner healing.

I had been to counseling for years. It was more like talk therapy; we never prayed together. When I finally found inner healing, we prayed through the sessions with Holy Spirit…This was after 11 years of me seeking counseling and help…and within ONE week of inner healing my heart was free!

I still experienced temptation but it wasn't coming from within; it was coming from without. My friend said that familiar spirits would try to come and lure me back into it, but I was able to resist it now.

Eventually, it all lifted. I now feel totally comfortable in my own body and when thoughts come, it's almost like trying to tell me to rob a bank. (In other words, it's not even a serious consideration or temptation.)

Wow. Linda has such an incredible story. We continued to chat for a while after that interview and I am grateful she made time to tell us her story.

Linda serves as Campus Pastor at Purdue University and is currently working on her Doctorate thesis. She is open about her story and seeks to help others find truth and freedom. Her testimony and both scientific and biblical discoveries on this topic can be found on her website. [31]

Chapter Nineteen

Firehouse Chronicle #3
Deborah

"Commit everything you do to the Lord. Trust him, and he will help you" (Psalm 37:5 NLT)

"Commit your works to the Lord [submit and trust them to Him], And your plans will succeed [if you respond to His will and guidance]" (Proverbs 16:3 AMP).

I believe we can pour out our hearts to God with honesty, authenticity, sorrow, and even travail. It is not wasted time; rather it can bear fruit. It did for me. The Lord has built my confidence in Him showing me that He is near to the broken-hearted (Psalm 34:18). He often hears and answers my questions and prayers in ways that are unique, delightful, and exceptional to experience. The beauty of relationship with the Lord, and the growth He provides, can be more apparent and manifest at different times in our lives. This third Firehouse Chronicle is one of those great times. This encounter also built my faith and increased my desire to know God and His Truth in a deeper way. It gives me such peace to know that I can bring complex and challenging issues to Him and then allow Him to point me to resources, information and answers.

I want to walk with Him into the future He has for me. I hope this encounter will challenge and inspire you—give or increase a longing in You to experience God and His messages so that you can better navigate the questions and issues of our lives. God is so personal and loves us so very much—more than we often think. He has a purpose for everything. God knows our longings.

"O Lord, all my longing is before you; my sighing is not hidden from you" (Psalm 38:9 ESV).

One morning I lay in bed weeping, telling the Lord all about the things I did not understand, and asking why after obeying Him in writing, "*The Elephant Gospel,*" and doing what I thought He wanted, my life looked so grim. Why did I feel like a failure? I begged God to give me something more to do that really mattered for His Kingdom. I felt sidelined, not amounting to much of anything and wondering if God thought of me the same way others had treated me. I poured out my heart in grief and sobbing.

Within a week of that weeping, crying out to God episode, the leader of a local ministry, (I had been attending their free prayer counseling sessions), called me and said that while he was praying, the Lord put it on his heart to call me and invite me to an event. He asked me to attend the first ever Mass Resistance Conference in Texas, also called Teens4Truth. He shared the details and invited me to have what would become my first book booth and official introduction as an author. I was to be interviewed and be a part of a team representing this local ministry. I was very excited and began reflecting on what God would have me say.

At about this same time, I was invited to go to Tennessee for a "LifeWay Leaders Conference". This conference was taking place the weekend before the Texas conference. It was the first time I would travel two weekends in a row for ministry events. It seemed God had answered my deepest desire and had activated me. I was excited to not only attend the Leaders Conference but also the "Mass Resistance Conference" in Texas.

On one of the days during the Leaders Conference, I was on my own at lunch. I ventured out to find a place to eat. I came across a Firehouse restaurant. I prayed, OK *Lord, this would be a 3 for 3 if you brought me an encounter here.* I looked around the restaurant and many fellow conference attendees were eating together. None were alone. I approached an empty table and sat down. I started eating and reached for the newspaper that had been left on the table where I sat. It was the Section B of USA TODAY 11/09/2017. At the bottom of the page my eyes landed on an article that was titled, "*German Records Must Allow Third Gender Option.*" The word *gender* caught my eye and I wondered what it was about. The subtitle was: "*Country Leads Europe in Recognizing Intersex.*" I wondered about this term: "intersex." So I began to read the article by Austin Davis, a Special for USA Today article.

"BERLIN - Your newborn could be registered as a boy, a girl or a different gender entirely if you live in Germany after the country's high court ruling Wednesday that lawmakers must recognize a 'third gender' from birth."

As I read this short article, I began to realize that perhaps this newspaper was my third Firehouse encounter. This time, though, the encounter was with myself and it involved critical questions of our day. After reading the article, I had so many questions and thoughts soaring through my head. From the title of the article, my impression was that **any** baby in Germany could be registered third gender. *Was this true? "Could **any baby** be registered third gender?" That did not make sense to me. What was intersex? How precisely is it defined? What is the underlying cause and basis for an intersex child? Is intersex rare in the United States? What is the comparison to cases in Germany? What is God doing in and through my life as a result of this article?*

On that day at Firehouse, I asked the Lord to teach me and show me what He wanted me to learn from this article. My career of many years was as an Obstetrics nurse, both full time, then part-time. I had never seen an intersex baby. Also, there was NEVER any question of the sex of a newborn. The sex of a baby was always very clear and obvious at delivery.

The article and the questions it caused brought my mind back many years, remembering the fact that as a child I thought at times I wanted to be a boy. I felt being a girl was inferior to being a boy. I felt my dad favored my brother over me and my two sisters. There were many factors in my young life that caused me to think being a boy would be a better, superior, safer, and more opportune life. I especially wanted to be stronger and better able to protect myself. Being a girl seemed weaker and less esteemed/respected/celebrated. I wanted to feel more valued and loved. If I had been born today and was given a choice, even as a minor, to change my sex, I may have chosen male at that young age. What would that have meant? I realize now that that choice would have been based on temporary feelings and perceptions I had as an 8 or 9 year old. Just thinking about it (the ramifications of such a misguided yet possible choice that I was too young and immature to make) made me queasy. I would have missed the delight of accepting and living out my true femininity and the joys of marriage and children and now grandchildren!

I felt so overwhelmed and saddened by the whole issue. I felt God's leading to understand this area more thoroughly. I sensed the importance of learning the world's views on these topics, but even more importantly what God's Word says regarding these issues. If even something as basic as the determination of the sex of a child can be distorted by the enemy, I believe we need to be prepared to confront the flood of confusion, chaos and immorality Satan seeks to usher in.

The memory of the first and only time I had ever *heard* of a child diagnosed as being "hermaphrodite" (it is my understanding this would be included within the term intersex today) was when I was in nursing school at the University of Florida, participating in a preceptor-ship with a Head Start Preschool Program. This child's care plan was addressed at a student nursing gathering that I attended. I had never heard of this diagnosis or known it was a possibility until being involved in discussing this child's care plan. The school system, the family and the nurses worked hard to understand how to best help the family and child in this difficult situation.

Then I thought of the memory of a recent phone conversation with a friend: she was concerned for her relative and was asking for prayer for her. The relative was a Christian kindergarten teacher in a public school. She had just been called by the principal of the school during the summer break and told, "There is a family that has a child who will be in your class this school year. The child is a female now but she will be having a sex change soon after school starts. So when school starts you are to call the child the boy's name they have chosen and are to address the child as a boy as soon as school starts." There was no other information about the child given to the teacher by the principal. The teacher needed prayer about how to handle this situation. She questioned if this was best for the child, especially at the child's young age. She wondered how it would affect other children in her class and how it interfaced with her own belief system.

Life is not simple in these matters. Issues like these cause us to pause and reflect. Is this the wave of the future? Did the little girl want this because of intersex birth or for other varied reasons such as a gender versus sex consideration? Why did both her parents so readily support her decision at such a young age? Would Christians treat this family with grace or judgment? Should they or would they ask the hard questions and resolve to help no matter the answers?

The world's morality changes with the culture. What is commonly acceptable today was unheard of, and even if heard of, radically disapproved of, in my childhood. Christ followers face the dilemma of living according to biblical principles and ethics, yet treating those living by the morality of our culture with grace, mercy, truth and kindness.

I was doing a lot of preparing and soul searching during the week preceding the Mass Resistance, Teens4Truth Conference. I thought about that newspaper article and how it had rocked my world. So many questions without clear answers; difficult dilemmas and horizons up ahead. But God is at work and has a plan and He revealed many detailed answers to my questions within a week.

I believe that my call in life is related to abortion, sexual abuse, sexual confusion, LGBTQs, and gender issues—and perhaps in ministry to youth in these areas. The Lord had obviously highlighted the three Firehouse Chronicles in my life and their relation to these issues. I wondered if even the name of the restaurant was significant and symbolic? [32]

I arrived at the Mass Resistance, Teen4Truth Conference and the booth next to the one I was assigned, belonged to Ellie Klipp. She wrote the children's book titled: *I Don't Have To Choose*. She and her husband and I conversed, and we exchanged books. Ellie and I connected in conversation and prayer and shared heart-to-heart. I was moved by her testimony. Nevertheless, I almost missed the answers I would be given through her, because of the reaction I had to a situation with protestors the next morning.

I arrived early that next morning and saw a mixed group of young men and women in front of the conference center. Most of those who picketed with signs appeared to be college and high school age. I stopped and talked to some of them. One picketer told me that most of those picketing were students from a nearby seminary that supports and allows homosexuals to be a part of the student body. As I was talking kindly and respectfully to one student, two men came up and began interacting with the protestors. The talk by the two men with the protestors got heated and sounded unloving and bashing. I asked them to please stop arguing. The men completely ignored me like I never spoke. Then I yelled, "Please stop! Without love we are nothing."

I felt so angry at the men for the way they seemed to address this group. As a result of their hostility and confrontational attitude, I felt more inclined to side with the protestors than the two men. These men appeared to be associated with the Mass Resistance conference, but at that point, I was not certain. However, I did know that if this was the resistance they wanted and supported, I wanted nothing to do with it. Because of the uncertainty of it all, I felt confused and questioned my continued attendance at the Mass Resistance conference. Yes, we are to stand up for righteousness but if we are not first living gospel love and acceptance (of people regardless if we disagree with their lifestyles), will our voices be heard, let alone will our voices matter? I believe the answer is no. Grace, truth and love are needed. Attacking beliefs by way of accusations and even biblical warnings, may not be the way to go about showing a group of protestors the real Jesus and His resistance to sin, especially when those protestors do not believe that their sexuality is a sin!

… but in your hearts honor Christ the Lord as holy, always being prepared to make a defense to anyone who asks you for a reason for the hope that is in you; yet do it with gentleness and respect,
(1 Peter 3:15 ESV)

I decided to press on in faith that God had brought me there and so I went to the conference hoping for more clarity and further insight on how to navigate these mind-fields (mine-fields) and differences. That afternoon Ellie gave an exceptional, professional, scientific presentation on many subjects related to sexuality, gender, and the like. Her talk included specific information on what intersex is, the known causes and the related gender issues. She also shared statistics on health consequences and suicidal rates after transgender surgery and many related teachings. She was truly a blessing to me. If you want to hear what Ellie presented, here is the link: https://www.massresistance.org/docs/gen3/17d/MR-TX-Teens4Truth-Conf-101817/presentations.html (Gender versus Gender Identity, Ellie Klipp)

I marveled at God's timing and answers to my questions. It was like God was teaching me and lining up these important insights. The information, teachings, and testimonies in the conference were fascinating. Such new and totally mind-blowing facts about what is and has been happening in America and the world. I did not know these issues existed at all, and I think most Americans have no idea about some of what we were taught either.

There is absolutely no question that we, in the world, should support, love and assist those children born as intersex. The intersex child has as much value, purpose and meaning as any other child. However, the existence of intersex children (estimated at between 0.5 and 1.7% of German newborns) does not change the Christian belief that God made us male and female. We do not want to add to the complexity and often pain of their situation by seeing others use them to validate and support lifestyles and world-views that are distinct from being intersex. An intersex child may need surgeries/hormones to help with establishing the child as male or female. This is not the same as a fully formed male or female wanting to change their sex and seeking medical help and procedures to effect this change. Intersex people are **not** typically the ones seeking transgender surgery as adults. [33]

Will this decision to use the term "third gender" by the German government, usher in more transgender ideology that could confuse a child's identity, rather than help establish it? **I wondered if people would now say, "See God did not make us male and female: intersex proves this."** Have intersex birth rates increased over the decades? How is this being used to fuel the enemy's agenda? Intersex is being called a third gender instead of being recognized as a unique and special physical condition as a result of malfunctions in the normal genetic growth process. (Intersex has been explained as a genetically based variance. In this sense it is not a third gender. It is a birth condition often requiring medical care.)

Will Christians go by what the Word of God says, namely that God made us male and female? He did not make a third gender, so will this terminology in the birth registration make it look like He did? Will Christians go by what is promoted in the culture by a minority worldview which strives to make specific fact patterns fit their beliefs? *Satan's challenge has always been "Did God really say?"* **When we veer from what God really did say we are in enemy territory. God said he made us male and female.**

So God created man in his own image,
in the image of God he created him;
male and female he created them. *(Genesis 1:27 ESV)*

In the process of writing this book, we did more research on these issues. It has become clear that the matter of intersex is incredibly complex and filled with a lot of emotion. We completely understand and agree with the desire of the German government to provide the parents of an intersex child with a way to complete a birth certificate in the most sensitive and accurate way. Providing a third option on a birth certificate would seem to be a good solution.

However, we believe that the problem could lie in the title that they are using for the registration since there is not a third sex or gender. This is an intersex birth not a third gender. The title of "third gender" opens the door to misinterpretations and untruths. In other words, the title of "third gender" being used for this registration is a potentially "bad" or confusing one. Using the two words "Third Gender," will be used to further the LGBTQ goals of recognizing non-binary sexual categories and promoting transgender procedures.

Even though the title of the article led us to believe all babies could be registered third gender, we determined by research that **only intersex births in Germany are given this third option.** Our concern is whether nations which adopt this registration terminology of "third gender" would ultimately extend the third option to all births and not just intersex births. Would it become commonplace that any parent could register any baby under the new registration so their children could choose their gender at any time in life? Could this be a goal that will be pursued by the LGBTQ community? Would they try to take advantage of this new birth registration, titled "third gender" that is in place in Germany for intersex population (0.5-1.7%) and extend this option to all births? These are crucial questions of our day and the next generations!

It became more apparent than ever, how critical it is that we be prepared to defend our faith and discern the lies of the enemy. The conference content was such that this verse seemed a reality: "Therefore, rejoice, O heavens and you who dwell in them! But woe to you, O earth and sea, for the devil has come down to you in great wrath, because he knows that his time is short!" (Revelation 12:12 ESV) The incredible need for God to rescue humanity from the course we are on was evident to me through all I learned at this conference. This verse came to my attention: "Rescue the perishing; don't hesitate to step in and help" (Proverbs 24:11 MSG).

Are we truly in the days of Noah? Just as in the days of Noah we need an Ark. That Ark today is Jesus Christ and the Cross. Jesus is the door and the Way to Truth and Life.

Our only hope is Jesus and His gospel being lived out and shared in the world.

Three examples of this type of life, a Christ-filled heart and life, desiring to step in and help rescue the perishing, are as follows:

1. The movie, *Audacity*, illustrates the above verses and highlights how one man made a difference by living true to the Gospel in these type "mine fields" and "mind fields". This movie is free on the web: audacitymovie.com or https://www.youtube.com/watch?v=tb-Pu2rtmDbY. It is a movie that provides an excellent gospel living model. Although many do not love as this man loved in the movie, it is given to show us our need to repent of hate and prejudice and begin to love like Christ loved us.

2. An illustration of the fullness of living true to the Gospel came known to me through a devotional (Day 93 One Year Bible 2019 by Nicky Gumble on You Version). Pope John Paul II experienced an attempted assassination by perpetrator Ali Agca. The Pope prayed for, publicly forgave, visited, became friends with Ali Agca and his family, and eventually asked for his pardoning in June of 2000. The Pope had almost died as a result of the shooting, and his health was never the same. At the Pope's death Agca and his family grieved because the Pope had been a great friend to them.

This is God's love and mercy! Jesus did even more for us than this! And when we have had a personal experience of Jesus and His Cross, we grow in Christ's ways and love, and His gospel fullness begins to manifest in our lives.

3. Another true story of living the way of the Cross is told in the book, *Shadow of the Almighty*. Jim Elliot, Nate Saint and three others formed a missionary team to the Acua Indians in Ecuador. All five were massacred by these Indians. Elisabeth Elliot and Rachel Saint (family of the martyred missionaries) went in and lived among the very Indians that killed their husband/family member! **Revival broke out** and transformations among the tribes were astounding. The Gospel was lived out in real time and its impact spread to affect the world. The LORD brought forth harvest in this ***martyrdom***. This well known and true story has been recounted in multiple writings and media presentations including a 2002 documentary called "*Beyond the Gates of Splendor*" and a 2005 film called "*End of The Spear*" spearheaded by Steve Saint, the son of Nate Saint, the martyred pilot.

Loving and forgiving those who hurt us and others is Christ-like and brings healing. However, the Holy Spirit needs to teach us when to lay down our lives for our enemies and when to stand up to them. We see in Christ's life that He did both. He knew how to defend Truth, to testify to the Truth and when and how to have victory by willingly laying down his life. But, loving our enemies does not mean we are to turn a blind eye to their crimes and allow them to continue in their sinful lives.

Do not say, "I will do to him as he has done to me; I will pay the man back for what he has done." The nature of the flesh to pay back evil for evil must be squelched. The wisdom and patience God gives will provide believers what is needed for this time and the future when we are in tune with His Spirit and obey His leadings. In the act of trusting God and forgiving self and others we can experience the greatness of Christ and His leading and f orgiveness (Proverbs 24:29: ESV).

"It's in Christ that we find out who we are and what we are living for. Long before we first heard of Christ and got our hopes up, he had his eye on us, had designs on us for glorious living, part of the overall purpose he is working out in everything and everyone. It's in Christ that you, once you heard the truth and believed it (this Message of your salvation), found yourselves home free—signed, sealed, and delivered by the Holy Spirit. This signet from God is the first installment on what's coming, a reminder that we'll get everything God has planned for us, a praising and glorious life" (Ephesians 1:11-14 MSG).

By this we know love, that he laid down his life for us, *and* ***we ought to lay down our lives for the brothers.*** *1 John 3:16 (ESV)*

The world needs the truth: "while we were still sinners Christ died for us" to be lived out in our lives to others. There may be times we are to be willing to die for the sinner to show the love of Christ. This is gospel love, gospel lifestyles. To live is Christ, to die is gain (Philippians 1:21).

Prayer

Lord, we pray for laborers for the harvest and for You to open the eyes and minds of many to see the truth of the gospel and be rescued from deception and destruction of sin. Please raise up writers and speakers, especially for the youth, to share Biblical truths in humility and with loving attitudes through the Holy Spirit's leadership. Please help Christian families and schools be true to Your Word and Gospel. Please help your people know how to love all people and how to show compassion, wisdom and caring even in the midst of "gender wars"! Teach us how to present these issues in truth, grace and love. Lord, help us be and stay true to what Your Word says: You are Creator and made us male and female. Help us to learn the facts of what causes intersex and not let media and other sources of information lead us away from the medical facts and biblical creation. May we be wise and loving in our conversations and sharing of facts. May we share our journeys as you lead us and learn to be discerning of how to share discreetly and in ways that show "love covers a multitude of sin" without detailing any sins that would not edify the hearer. May we be confident of our forgiveness through Christ and share the Good News with passion. Bring the wonder of your mercy forth and a greater desire to share Your message of salvation, rescue and transformation to Your people. Help us rescue the perishing and step in and help as you lead. Help us live true to "the preaching of the cross. Help us understand it is to them that perish foolishness; but unto us which are saved it is the power of God" (1 Corinthians 1:18 KJV). Make the preciousness of your Truths, as clearly reflected in Your Word, connect to our hearts as we are connected to You. Please equip us, grow our hearts in grace, and bring us to be willing to live the great commission in a greater measure. In Jesus' Name, Amen. [34]

Chapter Twenty

The Christian Marriage
Deborah

For this reason a man will leave his father and mother and be united to his wife, and the two will become one flesh. This is a profound mystery—but I am talking about Christ and the church. However, each one of you also must love his wife as he loves himself, and the wife must respect her husband" (Ephesians 5:31-33 NKJV).

Ephesians 4:2: "Be completely humble and gentle; be patient, bearing with one another in love."

For every Christian it is important to consider 1) how to live our faith out more fully and faithfully 2) how to successfully guard the virtue of chastity and purity as a part of the foundation of our faith, sexuality and life. In this next section, a few basic discussions on these topics will be addressed.

Since God made us and knows us better than we know ourselves, we can be confident in trusting Him, since He knows what is best. We can be certain of His teachings and commands. This is especially important when we are confronted by those who are living by the cultural morality of the world, especially those we love and who are closest to us. (It can be a challenge when relating directly with those closest to us.) Knowing how to be true to the teachings of Christ in our own life while speaking truth to others in an appealing, loving, magnetic way, will take the Holy Spirit and God's Word. It is important that we guard our faith while accepting the people who are living lifestyles directly opposed to our faith. Knowing and being IN God's Word is critical to our growth, obedience and faithfulness.

I would like to share an experience I had that caused me to stop and pause and see in a greater measure the importance that God's Word places on our sexuality and Christian marriage. Afterwards, I processed my thoughts by writing in my journal. I titled the entry: "The Bare Necessity of Guarding the Morality of Sex and Marriage":

Last evening for dinner, I had the joy and pleasure of meeting up with three high school classmates—one I had not seen for more than 40 years. We shared our lives with each other in openness and honesty. The time was refreshing and very encouraging, even though we spoke of how all of us have buried at least one parent, two of us both parents, and two who are in the process of "end of life" with a parent.

The time flew by quickly. It seemed we had only just sat down when we realized it was late and that we all needed to return to our respective homes. Looking back on life and sharing thoughts about our parent's death(s) and the process of experiencing the severity of these losses was a sobering, but also a spiritual conversation. It was a time of good fellowship.

I shared about the book I wrote, *The Elephant Gospel*. Each friend was gracious, kind and yet very surprised to hear what they did not know about me even though all knew me fairly well during high school and some even as early as 7th grade, both inside and outside of school.

At some point, I surprised myself by saying: "Sex is one thing that can wreak havoc, more than maybe any other thing in life. It can mess you up. And the church really does not often talk on this!" We all agreed and talked a bit on this subject. All this brought a realization of how important biblical sexuality is to all generations, especially the next generation.

When I got home to my husband, I enjoyed sharing the highlights of the evening. Then, as is our usual practice we read a chapter out of the Bible before bed and prayers together. The chapter we read together was Acts 15 in The Message Bible. (The Biblical passage is an important one because of the simple yet profound regulations listed and when observed, enabled unity between Jews and Gentiles. Please note the bolded words that address the foundational importance of Christian sexuality and marriage.)

"James broke the silence. 'Friends, listen.....

So here is my decision: We're not going to unnecessarily burden non-Jewish people who turn to the Master. We'll write them a letter and tell them, 'Be careful to not get involved in activities connected with idols, ***to guard the morality of sex and marriage ...*** *It seemed to the Holy Spirit and to us that you should not be saddled with any crushing burden, but* ***be responsible only for these bare necessities:*** *Be careful not to get involved in activities connected with idols; avoid serving food offensive to Jewish Christians (blood, for instance);* ***and guard the morality of sex***

***and marriage.** These guidelines are sufficient to keep relations congenial between us. And God be with you!'"* (Acts 15:13-21, 28-29).

The **bolded** words jumped off the page for me and stirred my heart: **the *bare necessity* of our Christian faith—"guarding the morality of sex and marriage are key foundations to our faith."**

These words truly impacted me because that very same morning, I had asked God to make His Will real to me and lived out in my life. I saw clearly that guarding marriage and our intimacy is God's Will for me. I vowed to make my marriage more of a priority and a joy and to be an example for our children and to others as well. The Lord seemed to impress this truth with impact on me many times. How to love the Lord as my first love and my husband as my second love is something I consider and try to live. The fact we are still married and love each other as we do is by God's grace. For this I am eternally grateful. It is surely an act of God.

Perhaps this question is for every Christian: how do we uphold and guard the morality of sex and marriage? I believe it starts with our hearts. Where our hearts are is where our truest treasure will be and our hearts determine the course of our lives (Matthew 6:21; Proverbs 4:23). When we make the LORD our treasure and our first love, everything flows from His love and goodness. Guarding our hearts and praying for The LORD to be our first love is essential.

When The LORD is our first love our foundation is secure and "our house" will be built on His Rock. We need to honor God by loving well (1 Corinthians 13). Also our devotion to God should govern and be reflected in our sexuality. This means being chaste (abstaining from extramarital sex), and pure, whether married or single. (Many were hurt by the way "chastity" was presented to them in their youth. Whenever rules and religion dominate relationship and real love, hurt always seems to result.) [35] [36]

Christlikeness comes through abiding not striving. We need to seek the Holy Spirit's guidance about how to be active participants of victory in Christ in the midst of the cultural war in America within us and around us. The challenges are great with rampant in your face pornography, abortion on demand and LGBTQ "politically correct" media blitzes bombarding us almost continuously.

Even the youngest children in society and in schools are being impacted. With the definition of marriage being turned upside down, and same sex marriage being legalized, accepted and promoted as a "new way of life" in America—we must take all of this to heart and get involved. By the leading of the Holy Spirit we need to be willing to take action with much prayer, to establish and guard the morality of sex and marriage in this, God's world.

I often wonder, why this subject of Biblical sexuality and Biblical marriage are not more clearly and effectively addressed in many Christian churches and schools?

One of the best sermons I have heard on marriage was by Dr. Timothy Keller. In that sermon,[37] Dr. Keller said, "The Bible says that the purpose of marriage is gospel reenactment." When I heard those words, I thought, *that is my marriage.* If ever we see the gospel, it is in our marriages. Only God could do what He has done in and with us as we forgive, accept and love another.

Spirit-Guided Relationships: Wives and Husbands
21 And further, submit to one another out of reverence for Christ.
25 For husbands, this means love your wives, just as Christ loved the church. He gave up his life
for her 26 to make her holy and clean, washed by the cleansing of God's word.[b] 27 He did this to
present her to himself as a glorious church without a spot or wrinkle or any other blemish. Instead,
she will be holy and without fault. 28 In the same way, husbands ought to love their wives as they
love their own bodies. For a man who loves his wife actually shows love for himself. 29 No one
hates his own body but feeds and cares for it, just as Christ cares for the church. 30 And we are
members of his body. (Ephesians 5:21, 25-29 NLT)

Prayer

LORD, help us experience You as the most valuable treasure on earth! Your constant love is better than life itself (Psalm 63:3a). Help us respond to Your love by loving You with all our heart, soul, mind, strength and also love our neighbor as ourselves. Help us love like Christ loved us starting in our marriages and families. Your New Covenant offers us hope. Help us live truer to the power in the cross to solve the world's problems. Help us, as Christians, to use the power in the Cross, boasting only on Christ crucified, as Paul did, to reverse the course of our generation's culture. Help us bring forth the truth of your Biblical teachings in loving ways that are more understandable, acceptable, and attractive to youth, not in wounding or manipulative methods. Help us teach parents and their children more on the importance of the morality in sex and marriage. May we provide many examples of married couples that live true to a loving, healthy, gospel marriage. In Jesus' Name, Amen

Chapter Twenty-One

Firehouse Chronicle #4
Richard and Deborah

"For by grace you have been saved through faith. And this is not your own doing; it is the gift of God" (Ephesians 2:8).

He saved us, not because of any works of righteousness that we have done, but because of His own compassion and mercy, by the cleansing of the new birth (spiritual transformation, regeneration) and renewing by the Holy Spirit, (Titus 3:5 AMP).

One of our goals in writing this book is to encourage the reader to truly reflect upon and seek guidance from his/her relationship with the Lord and Savior. The richness that is available to all of us by way of this relationship, is boundless. We truly believe in Romans 8:28 that God can work good in all things in our life, if we love Him and are called according to His purpose. We can gain from every experience if we earnestly seek Him - every experience! We can then begin to be used by the Lord to witness and share with others. This witness must be founded on the truth of what Christ has done though. There are definitely many times when we can move forward in doing what may seem good and right, but if we do not do these things as unto the Lord, and to honor and glorify his wonderful Name, then our actions really have no eternal value. Such is what we learned, believe it or not, from Firehouse Chronicle #4.

At the beginning of this year we traveled to visit our son and his wife, who live in another state. We arrived in their city around lunchtime. We called and asked for their recommendation as to what we could pick up for all of us to eat. They recommended we pick up subs at Firehouse. They did not know anything about our history with Firehouse or any of the content of our writing. (This book was still a work in progress at that time.) My husband and I were excited about their recommendation of Firehouse. We wondered if we might have a fourth kind of encounter.

Our time in the restaurant was uneventful. However, just getting Firehouse had me on alert and asking for God to speak to us. Consequently, I feel like we were more sensitive to what the Lord might be doing, through the leading of His Holy Spirit. It even caused me to think back to that very morning's conversation that I had with my husband.

My husband and I shared something with each other that we had never shared before. It was something we were each experiencing at the same time but without the other knowing about the depth of our respective experiences until we voiced them. We surprised each other. I don't recall who shared first, however, the substance of our sharing was the fact we both were concerned about, and fragile regarding, our serious heart and health issues. We were both reflecting on the possibility of death. Neither of us knew what the other was experiencing, though. I felt we had both aged significantly because of our individual conditions. This was a significant part of our mindset as we met with our son and our daughter in law, at their home.

After we had eaten our subs, our son asked us to watch a movie with him called "*Seven Pounds*". We had no idea what the movie was about, just that our son had seen it before and liked it and thought we would also. Our son did not know anything about the discussion that my husband and I had that very morning.

The movie began with the main character, Ben, narrating "How God created the world in seven days, and how he (Ben) managed to destroy his own in seven seconds". From that point, the mystery was on. As we watched the movie, there was a definite connection for us with our morning conversation! The movie ended with "the giving of a heart for the life of another" (literally). It was a deep movie with lots of emotion and sadness. It was not a predictable movie at all. It took us most of the movie to really figure out what was happening. Ben had a dark secret in his past that compelled him to commit seven significant acts of "kindness". He did this through self-sacrifices, to change the lives of seven people. Ben handpicked these seven as he felt they were both "worthy" and "good". The theme of restitution and working to forgive oneself by trying to make up for the debt owed due to one's actions and consequences, is an underlying, yet unspoken, foundational part of the movie.

After the movie, our son asked us how we liked it. My response was basically that I understood and identified with Ben. "I get it! I have lived that way to some degree myself. It is hard for a person to forgive themselves. It has been hard for me to forgive myself."

Nonetheless, when it was all said and done, the movie brought the following to our minds, which we believe created the substance of God's teaching us in Firehouse Chronicle #4:

1. Sometimes we get to the end of life (or the end of a hallway, see below) and the end result is not what we expect or thought it would be. The path we have taken has ended and it is a path we regret to have taken.

This reminded me of a serious blunder I made with this very son when he was still at an impressionable age, in about middle school. We attended a church play together. I should say, I pushed him to go with me. He did not want to go. (This was my first mistake— being a bully about religion.) Anyway, we got to the play, which was called "Heaven's Gates or Hell's Flames". It was an evangelistic drama.

There was a long line to enter the Church to see the play, and my son did not want to wait. It was not like me to cut a line and I am ashamed to admit it but I said,"Let's go this way!" I saw another hallway into the Church and there was no line at all. Guess what, there was a reason why there was no line down the hallway that I was taking us. Taking that hallway caused us to miss the entire play. You see, the line that we were in originally, was a line that passed through the church along a specific path. At various points in the church along that path, various scenes in the play were presented, with the ultimate scene being the Cross of Christ. **The way that I took us, completely bypassed the entire play, most importantly the Cross of Christ! We got to the end of the play, without having experienced the Cross at all.** I had cheated my son of really seeing and experiencing the Cross of Christ, the real way to Heaven's Gates. I feel grief just thinking of the error and wrong path and modeling I lived to our son. I realize in hindsight I was living "my way," down the wrong hallway, bypassing Christ and His Cross in my life at that time! I was determined to show our sons the way to Jesus but showed them the wrong way and missed Jesus at times!

This brings home the importance that as we witness to others, we do not want to guide them on a path that will bypass the cross of Christ. A life without Christ is meaningless and does not allow for the forgiveness of sins, thus it lacks any eternal value. Those taking a path that does not lead to the Cross may think they are doing just fine and avoiding problems, even paying their own debts, but it is a dead end path.

2. The sense of what is right and wrong is within all of us. We all know this instinctively. Further, when there is a wrong, our inner sense of justice demands that the wrong be made right. Since these senses were placed in our heart by our Heavenly Father, we should know that we need Him to be involved in every attempt to make a wrong, right. If our heart is misguided in these actions, by not seeking God's will and direction, there is no eternal value no

matter how good the actions may appear to the world. Without God, we, ourselves, become the god overseeing the actions and that can never be the best way. We want and need the One that is omniscient and omnipotent. Why would we seek to have anyone else as our Guide?

This movie gave us the awareness that the greatest wrong in our individual lives is the wrong we have committed against God. Ben in the movie recognized the wrong he had committed against his fellow man, and he was absolutely and completely driven to make it right. It would be our hope that we all see the truth about the wrong that we have committed against God and our fellowman by our disobedience and pride and then with that realization and conviction, be moved to restitution and seek restoration with the Father and then others as needed. However, no matter how much drive we have, the only way to the Father is through the Son, Jesus Christ. May our drive be to repent of our sin, accept Jesus as our Lord and Savior and recognize what He did for us on the Cross. May we have the drive to follow that path and be used by God to help many others to join us.

It is evident to me that Ben did not understand God's way of making people right with Himself: *"For they don't understand God's way of making people right with himself. Refusing to accept God's way, they cling to their own way of getting right with God by trying to keep the law" Romans 10:3 NLT.*

We can never pay back our sin debt to God. It is too great. Christ is the only One who can pay that debt and He did. If we try on our own and never receive what was fully given to us as a gift, we could die in vain without the true forgiveness and gift we were offered. The movie was grievous in that Ben did not know or rely on God's forgiveness! It reminded me of myself in my past, going about doing good but missing the Good that was done for me and offered to me through Christ. Once we have received the payment for our debts and the forgiveness of our sins…we have the greatest gifts on earth through the greatest treasure on earth: Jesus Christ! The magnitude of God's forgiveness is astounding! Such Good News! Our forgiveness has been (past tense) fully paid by Christ! We need not try to pay! We never could fully pay. Biblically, it is totally impossible to atone for our own sins through our actions! This is the Good News of Jesus! It inspired me to want to shout out Christ's great gift of forgiveness. To warn people not to live like Ben but live forgiven because of Christ.

Prayer

Dear LORD, help us know Christ's atonement is enough! Help us give up trying to self-atone. Help us recognize the futility of "trying to earn forgiveness". Help us to look to You for direction as to how to go back and make amends to those we have harmed as You lead us. Help us recognize restitution is Biblical (Leviticus 24:17-21; Numbers 5:6-7; Luke

19:8-9 and other verses). Help us ask for forgiveness from You and others when needed. We want to open our hearts. Help us "give our hearts" if you lead, to be vessels for You, Lord, so others can live: not to attempt to earn salvation for ourselves but to show the salvation/ gospel message in real time living! Real love sacrifices. Real love gives of self for the good of another. Real love is giving love for the other person's good not for selfish reasons. Real love is Christ-like. Real love changes the world. Real love is God honoring and not self honoring. Let us be a world changer, please LORD! LORD help our lives SHOUT Your forgiveness and love all because of JESUS! In Jesus' Name, Amen. [38]

Chapter Twenty-Two

A Prayer For A Second Chance
Deborah Mott

"But you will receive power when the Holy Spirit has come upon you, and you will be my witnesses in Jerusalem and in all Judea and Samaria, and to the end of the earth" (Acts 1:8).

"Imagine yourself as a living house. God comes in to rebuild that house. At first, perhaps, you can understand what He is doing. He is getting the drains right and stopping the leaks in the roof and so on; you knew that those jobs needed doing and so you are not surprised. But presently He starts knocking the house about in a way that hurts abominably and does not seem to make any sense. What on earth is He up to? The explanation is that He is building quite a different house from the one you thought of–throwing out a new wing here, putting on an extra floor there, running up towers, making courtyards. You thought you were being made into a decent little cottage: but He is building a palace. He intends to come and live in it Himself." - C.S. Lewis, Mere Christianity

In December of 2012, I had spinal surgery on my cervical (neck) area. The surgery experience helped me understand how God gives us second chances not only in our physical health but in opportunities to share His love and second chances in growing in spiritual health and maturity. [39]

I looked normal on the outside but on the inside I was a mess due to past incidents in my life. I desperately needed a physical re-alignment like I also needed a spiritual one! I needed a complete over-haul and reconstruction—a re-alignment from how I was crooked physically from multiple abuses and accidents, and spiritually mis-aligned from rejections, fears, and the burden of self-work, to a radical realignment with God's truth and abiding. I needed Christ and the New Covenant to take center stage and control in all aspects of my life.

My transformations came with suffering. Struggles with what I really believed began to emerge. The difference between religion that doesn't work and a real relationship with Jesus, (New Covenant), that does work, became evident. **I realized that although I was born-again, (in covenant with God through Christ) I was living more out of attempting to earn my salvation than *living from it.* Living from salvation is the way of real Christianity (Believe, SAVED, Obey)**! Living in the power of the Holy Spirit, not my own power, comes about by living from salvation and depending on Christ.

Just as the doctors examined me physically to prepare me for surgery, I needed to examine myself to prepare myself for spiritual reconstruction. God impressed upon me that what was taking place within me, was what I needed. It was also needed in many of His people.

The Bible tells us about Israel and several specific people who faced examination. Let's consider Saul, whose name changed to Paul, and Judas who betrayed Jesus.

Saul was a fanatically religious man, one who had missed Jesus entirely. Yet, Saul thought Christians had missed God by following Jesus. Saul uttered "threats with every breath and was eager to kill the Lord's followers" (Acts 9:1 NLT) because these people didn't follow his strict religious rules. But on the Damascus Road, Jesus confronted Saul with the truth. Saul was persecuting the Son of God. Jesus saved Saul and changed his name to Paul. From that moment on, Paul led people to the life-giving salvation of Jesus, started many churches, and wrote most of the New Testament through the inspiration of the Holy Spirit. Paul's confrontation with Jesus changed his life of zeal and determination for the sake of his religion to a man who had a personal and powerful covenant relationship with Jesus Christ.

"Imagine if a former member of ISIS ended up as the Pope and you'll be close to understanding what happened to the apostle Paul." [40]

The reason he changed is due to his encounter with Christ (Acts 9). What Paul experienced is exactly what Jesus said to Nicodemus in John 3, "You must be born again." After the Damascus Road, Paul's life reflected that he began to believe in Jesus as the Christ and Lord, and accepted a new covenant relationship with Jesus Christ. Paul had been a calloused, murderous opponent of "Christians". His changed heart - born of God's Spirit - transformed him to be a great apostle. He proclaimed Jesus as the Son of God, the Messiah. God anointed Paul to bring forth the Gospel to change the world.

Paul's life is living proof of his repentance and transformation through Christ and the fact that God can change any human heart. Later, Paul would write about the circumcision of the heart, by the Spirit (Romans 2:29). Paul was an advocate for Christ in marvelous and masterful ways. Paul stood for the true Gospel and protected the Gospel from enemies of the

Cross, (like he had been, and like Judaizers were) who pressured Christian leaders to conform to the letter of the law as the way of salvation. In Galatians 2:11-14 Paul corrects Peter. Peter was being pressured and influenced by the Judaizers. Paul warned that the Judaizers were "enemies of the cross". Paul compelled all believers to obey the truth that is in the Good News and to not fall away into the legalism of trying to earn salvation by self-works. Salvation is by faith and grace alone! Paul determined to boast only on Christ Crucified, Christ's Cross, as he testified to his own weaknesses and gave testimony of his sinful, murderous past. He wanted to show all those who were as he had been, the mystery and transformational power and epic greatness of the cross and resurrection of Jesus Christ.

****

Judas Iscariot was one of the twelve apostles—the elite group who traveled and ministered with Jesus. Judas was sent out with the other apostles, performing signs and wonders. For approximately three years, Judas ate and did life with Jesus and the other apostles. He even attended the Last Supper and allowed Jesus to wash his feet. But being with and interacting with other believers and even with Jesus Himself, will not necessarily make us believers. Satan entered Judas. (Matthew 10:4-15; John 6:70; Luke 22:3). Judas was eyewitness to the Deity of Christ! Jesus showed his power and love, showed him the way, offered mercy to Judas over and over. Jesus washed Judas' feet, and called him "friend," giving him a last chance, but Judas never received Christ as Lord. He did not enter into covenant with Jesus. Judas was a betrayer. Judas was a thief. His heart did not belong to Christ. All Judas' earlier outward good works meant nothing compared with his inward unchanged state. He failed to receive Christ despite being with Christ.

On the outside, it appeared that Judas was a true follower of Christ. We, too, can appear to be Christians. We may even do great deeds, supposedly in the name of Christ, but a personal and covenant relationship with Him is the only way of eternal life. We are offered this "gift of God" through Christ, then we receive His covenant indwelling. But people reject Christ. Jesus' words in Matthew 7:21-23 reflect Judas' dead state (See also Ephesians 2:1,5; Colossians 2:13: John 15:5; John 3:3, 7, 16, 36, 6:44,17:3). Sadly, there are many like him who never truly enter into new covenant relationship. We must believe In Christ and accept Christ's gift of forgiveness to know Christ (born again) in covenant.

"Examine yourselves, to see whether you are in the faith. Test yourselves. Or do you not realize this about yourselves, that Jesus Christ is in you?" (2 Corinthians 13:5 ESV).

"Not everyone who says to me, 'Lord, Lord' will enter into the kingdom of heaven, but the one who does the will of my Father who is in heaven. On that day many will say to me, Lord, Lord, did we not prophesy in your name, and cast out demons in your name, and do many mighty works in your name? And then will I declare to them, 'I never knew you; depart from me, you workers of lawlessness'" (Matthew 7:21-23 ESV).

Religion without intimate COVENANT relationship is woefully empty in itself and is simply following rules while pretending to belong to God. This is a counterfeit, a Judas, and in the end if there is no change, Jesus will say, 'I never knew you. Away from me, you evil-doers!'" (Matthew 7:21-23 NIV) How sad! May this never be said to any of us.

Jesus answered him, "Truly, truly, I say to you, unless one is born again he cannot see the kingdom of God" (John 3:3 ESV).

"Let us examine and probe our ways, And let us return to the Lord" (Lamentations 3:40).

Prayer

LORD, Draw us to fully receive Christ and His love. Help people be true to "know Christ" by faith and grace being recipients of the works of Christ. Help us understand there is no greater friend than Christ and ward off enemies of His Cross! LORD help us be like Paul in our fervency to live and defend the true Gospel and not let legalizers pressure or influence us away from relationship with Jesus and into the false assurance of being rule-followers! Help us be Christ believers, Christ followers and Christ faithful to our last breaths out of love and gratitude for what Christ has done for and in us! God help us protect Your Gospel and help send "a Paul" to us if we revert back to self-works to wake us up to the offense this is to Christ and to the wasted-ness of living legalistically and not wholly committed to live Christ (Philippians 1:21) and proclaim Christ. Help us also pray as Paul prayed to open the eyes of those who do not know Jesus. To lead them from darkness to light, from the power of Satan to God, that they may receive forgiveness of sins, and a place among those who are sanctified by faith (Acts 26:18). Help us to do all we can to uphold Christ and make His Gospel fully known and the valuable, Good News it is! LORD, help us learn from the rejection, betrayal, foolishness and apostasy of Judas. Help us recognize that to reject Christ is disastrous. Help us know a life rejecting a covenant relationship with You is a wasted life (Matthew 26:24; Mark 14:21). Again, please help many be willing to receive Jesus, be loyal to You, Lord, and help us love You with our first love always. In Jesus' Name, Amen.

Chapter Twenty-Three

Pre-Op and Second Chance Realized
Deborah Mott

And ***this is eternal life, that they know you, the only true God, and Jesus Christ*** *whom you have sent (John 17:3 ESV my emphasis).*

"Let not your hearts be troubled. Believe in God; believe also in me. ***2*** *In my Father's house are many rooms. If it were not so, would I have told you that I go to prepare a place for you?* ***3*** *And if I go and prepare a place for you, I will come again and will take you to myself, that where I am you may be also" (John 14:1-3 ESV).*

I entered the multi-level garage where I would park, grateful to arrive on time without getting lost in the surrounding metropolis or the vast medical complex where my appointment awaited. I sighed with relief.

In the garage, I noticed a father helping his daughter, who was in a wheelchair, as they began the trek to whatever appointment awaited them. They took the elevator. I took the stairs. Strangely, we arrived at the office destination at almost the same time. This office was a very long distance from where we parked, and I marveled at the timing. Later I would feel the indelible mark which my brief experiences with these two people would leave on me.

My appointments were multi-leveled and multi-location-ed. The day was like no other day I had ever lived.

I felt that in completing the pre-operative registration and its many informational and procedural requirements, I was potentially placing my life at risk, all in the hope of being normal on the inside. During this pre-op process, I was told about some scary possible outcomes. I might be in ICU. I might awaken with no voice or hoarseness, which might or might not be temporary. I might be bound to a wheelchair for the rest of my life, or worst of all, I might die. I signed the surgical consent to treatment and chose to trust my life to the hands of the surgeons and medical team, believing/knowing Christ was anchoring me.

I sat near the girl and her father in the pre-op waiting room. She looked as if her life hung in the balance, but clearly and sadly, more treatment was ahead for her. I had immediate compassion for her. I gave her what I hoped was a brave smile, a silent urging of courage for whatever we both were to undergo.

Most people in the waiting room had obvious serious conditions, as did the girl. I wanted to speak with her to comfort her, but I just could not find the words to share. All the words which came to my mind, seemed so inadequate. She appeared battle worn, with sparse hair and sad, hollow eyes. I looked normal on the outside. I related to her but felt she could not relate to me. We appeared to be at the polar ends of the health spectrum.

Throughout the long pre-op day, we kept seeing each other in various departments of the hospital, usually at a distance. We never talked although I longed to speak to her.

During the week that followed that pre-op day, I often thought of her, and said, "arrow prayers" for her. One that I remember was: "Lord, if You want me to talk to her give me a second chance."

The day of the biggest surgery of my life came early. We left our house while it was still dark, before 4 am. My surgery was a C4-7 laminectomy. For non-medicals, my upper spinal cord was being compressed/endangered from the misaligned vertebrae and needed reconstruction and realignment.

As my husband and I traveled in the dark, I felt God's hand of assurance. We entered the waiting area ahead of our appointment time. There was only one couple there. Then as time drew near for the surgery registration area to open, I was stunned by the number of people arriving and queuing up for surgery. It felt eerie, like cattle being led to a slaughter. I felt such compassion, realizing that every day people are undergoing surgeries of this magnitude. So many people were hurting, even close to death. They were willing to accept surgery, though, in an attempt to improve or lengthen their life. Like me. All of us willing to risk a lot, for another chance at life.

Suffering is difficult to face and watch even when you are a believer. Jesus is the Great Physician, yet so many people are hurting. *What could I say or do to make any difference? I wanted my faith to do some good. Why hadn't Jesus healed these people? Why hadn't he healed me?*

My lengthy surgery was a success. I woke up with both arms free of the nerve pain that had plagued me, along with strength in my arms and hands. I could also talk. I was happy for a good outcome, but was in the most grueling and intense pain I have ever experienced and with a confining and awkward neck brace on. I arrived by stretcher to my room from the post-op area.

My husband was already in my room, along with my mom and sister. Deep appreciation welled in me for their presence. My husband was immediately at my side. My heart felt relief. My mouth was so dry. It was hard to talk. I asked for water. My first swallows choked me, and I began coughing and crying. My mom and sister cried with me. I must have been a sight. Later they told me how pale and ghostly I had appeared. (Having the neck brace on heightened my reality of the seriousness of it all.) We were all scared. My life still felt like it hung in the balance.

I was originally thankful that I had not been taken to ICU after the surgery. However, that evening, when I was told I would have to get on a stretcher and go to X-ray, I longed to be in ICU, where X-ray would have come to me. I could not fathom having to endure the transfer to a gurney and being wheeled through the hospital. I wept and said to my husband, "Why is this expected of me? It is too much. I cannot do it." It took my husband awhile to calm me and for my tears to cease. I wondered, *Where is God? Why would He allow me to suffer so much?* I felt depressed and abandoned.

As I arrived at X-ray, my pain had worsened due to the transfer, and the bumps and jolts of the trip. But when I saw the girl and her father, I understood that God was giving me my second chance. I was filled with genuine joy at the sight of them. The grace of God empowered me, and I said, "I am so happy to see you again. I prayed for you this week and asked the Lord if He wanted me to talk to you, He would give me another chance. So here you are because He loves you so much."

She looked at me surprised and a bit suspicious, as if to silently ask how I could say those things, just look at us… with both of us in pain, and after undergoing surgery. I knew we were now "on level ground" as I was no longer the picture of health.

I asked, **"Do you know Jesus?"**

She said, "I never got into church much."

I said, "That is okay, some churches will actually lead you away from Him. ***What is important is to know Jesus. Try talking to Him. He is there for you and wants a relationship with you."*** (Saying the first statement felt right because of the tone she used in saying, "I never got into church much". Plus it was my experience to some degree and sadly the way I too had led others away from Him, not even meaning to do so! I mean no offense to any reader or church. I, in no way, am trying to bash the church or imply that all or most churches are guilty of this! I realize the true church is Christ's Bride. But the fact is there are churches that do not make relationship with Christ and the offer of forgiveness of sin through His work alone, known.)

I wanted to say more but the orderly wheeled me away and into the X-ray room from the hallway. I believe God sometimes gives second chances like this, like He did for me, especially when there is an opportunity to share His love, even in such a brief and simple way. I truly thank God for giving me this second chance.

"This is how we know we're living steadily and deeply in him, and he in us: He's given us life from his life, from his very own Spirit. Also, we've seen for ourselves and continue to state openly that the Father sent his Son as Savior of the world. Everyone who confesses that Jesus is God's Son participates continuously in an intimate relationship with God. We know it so well, we've embraced it heart and soul, this love that comes from God" (1 John 4:13-16 MSG).

When you pass through the waters, I will be with you;

and through the rivers, they shall not overwhelm you;

when you walk through fire you shall not be burned,

and the flame shall not consume you (Isaiah 43:2 ESV).

Prayer

LORD, we who are in covenant with You, please fill us with Your words to share with those who do not know You. Help us know your timing and be prayerful and ready to give out the living hope You have given to us! No matter where we find ourselves, help us pray for those around us and allow any suffering we experience to be used to purify us to be a truer light of Your gospel. Thank you for the promise that hearts can be changed by You. Increase our compassion for others, establish our hearts, put some heart encouragement into us, your servants, especially during times of affliction and discouragement. Cause us to be won over by Your heart. Thank You we are One in You. Teach us how to rejoice in our sufferings as they can lead to endurance and character and produce hope and hope does not put us to shame because Your love has been poured into our hearts through the Holy Spirit who has been given to us. (Romans 5:3-5) Let our reasonableness, our gentleness, be known to all, for You are near (Philippians 4:5). Help us cope when life feels unfair but have faith that You, Lord God, are always good. (Psalm 73:1). Help us make the most of every opportunity because we know there is salvation in Christ alone and the time is short (Revelation 22:12).

There is no salvation in any other name (Acts 4:12). Help us keep crying out to You and help us be faithful to You LORD and **be willing to trust You** when life hurts! Please bring in a 100-fold-harvest in our lives (Matthew 13:23), In Jesus' Name, Amen.

Chapter Twenty-Four

Telling Our Story
Deborah

May God be gracious to us and bless us

and make his face to shine upon us, Selah

that your way may be known on earth,

your saving power among all nations *(Psalm 67:1-2 ESV).*

I have told the glad news of deliverance in the great congregation; behold, I have not restrained my lips, as you know, O Lord. I have not hidden your deliverance within my heart; I have spoken of your faithfulness and your salvation; I have not concealed your steadfast love and your faithfulness from the great congregation. As for you, O Lord, you will not restrain your mercy from me; your steadfast love and your faithfulness will ever preserve me (Psalm 40:9-11 ESV).

When Jesus came to earth, He became like us...fully human but remained fully God. Yet He experienced life the same way we experience life. He knew pain and suffering, and He felt rejection. When I consider the magnitude of what Jesus lived and died to give me, I want others to know Jesus.

I spoke to the girl because I wanted her to have the full, beautiful and eternal life that Jesus offers and which starts upon receiving Him. I wanted her to know salvation, be a member of Christ's family, if she were to die. I didn't know how long she had. I wanted her to have hope and love, not just from her earthly father who seemed so faithful, but from our amazing Heavenly Father! Faith in Christ makes all the difference because He is the way to heaven and is hope, for any who will believe.

No words can express the joy and goodness of having the Holy Spirit empower me to share with this girl and her father. The joy I experienced in meeting up with them and giving my brief statements, in the power of the Holy Spirit, was amazing. I sensed the Lord in all of this. I would gladly go through all the fear, pain and uncertainty of this surgery experience again, just to provide an opportunity to share with the girl and her father. Just as we found ourselves at the same destination on numerous occasions, I also wanted them to end up at the ultimate destination: Heaven. It is such a release, a cleansing, a purification of life, to share the greatness of the hope and gift of God!

I believe that this hospital experience confirms the **most important call of my life** (and really that of all believers): **to share the truth of Christ, that by faith in Him there is grace for salvation. We believers are to protect the Gospel from enemies of the Cross, to uphold the true Gospel, to live and preach Christ crucified and risen for the forgiveness of sin. Believe. Saved. Obey.** (The true Gospel is in that order alone!) We are to repent where we have not lived the true Gospel. (In other words: "Obey before saved living" is a false gospel life.) We are to return to Christ for the forgiveness of our sins. **Christ's blood purchased our redemption**. (1 Peter 1:18-19; Ephesians 1:7-8) **Being born again by Christ's work alone is Good News.** He has called believers to share His Good News. Jesus has overcome the world (John 16:33) and we are to overcome by believing and living His overcoming as Revelation 12:11 states!

And they overcame him because of the blood of the Lamb and because of the word of their testimony, and they did not love their life even when faced with death (Revelation 12:11 NASB).

"The greatest part of telling others about the Lord is that you now have the opportunity to affect the lives of others for good; now they will have the chance to come to know Christ as their Savior. The great blessing that is in your life can be shared with someone else to bring him or her hope. If the desolate and downtrodden woman at the well could be a witness, certainly you and I can do the same. 'Then, leaving her water jar, the woman went back to the town and said to the people, Come, see a man who told me everything I ever did. Could this be the Christ?'" (John 4:28-29 NIV) [41]

Our joy and our purpose is to use the opportunities God gives to us to tell others about His love and His salvation. We want to use our stories, (like the woman at the well did in telling the townspeople) to help others! Once we have received Christ's forgiveness and realize the greatness of the removal of our guilt, as far as the East is from the West, we can accept that God does not remember our sins, or hold them against us.

However, we will still know the horror of the sin itself. The hope is that this will motivate us to protect others from doing what we did. But even if they do what we did, we know there is Someone stronger than the power of sin and the grave. His love never fails and His forgiveness is available! The greatness of what we received from Christ is what we want for others! We are shouting out about the LORD's Great Love and Forgiveness and Power to heal because we have received it and know the Goodness of God!

When we are motivated to speak up and help others consider the choices they have before them, and the eternal consequences of those choices, it helps us to believe that God is bringing good out of the worst of our sins. Every time we confess our sin, it helps others realize the healing that comes with our confession. The Light of Christ shines on those past secret sins that have kept us in bondage and not living true to the Gospel Greatness. It gives great glory to God (makes Him Known and welcomed) when we share His message of hope and life with others. God's grace is absolutely astounding! Giving glory to God is to make His greatness known so others can know His greatness! We point to Christ and His great Salvation! We share how God delights to accept our repentant hearts and FORGIVE SIN - make us whole in Him again!

Another friend, Angela, has this testimony and gave me permission to share: "My Dad prayed Psalm 67:1 over me frequently. I remember him praying "May God be gracious to you and bless you and may His face shine on you." I often pray the same prayer over my children as I put them to bed, thinking of my Dad and wanting to pass on that blessing to my children. I recently read the verse after this prayer in Psalm 67:2 NIV, and realized there is more to the prayer. There is a reason why we pray for this blessing. It is so that **God's ways and salvation would be known among the nations.** I am going to start praying the second verse over my kids too! *That they would be blessed and have His face shine on them* ***so that*** **your ways may be known on earth, your salvation among all nations.** What a powerful and beautiful prayer!"

We want salvation among the nations when we have experienced God's goodness. God gave me a spiritual second chance and a physical second chance. He is the God of the second chance. My hope and prayer are that my second chance meeting offered life in Christ to the girl and her father. My second chance surgery offered a new physical level of life to me while symbolically representing to me **what the LORD wanted to do within and through me, and within and through His Church.** These experiences helped me to greater identify with Jesus and receive a testimony of gospel proportions that flooded over me. The experience brought purpose to my pain as it changed my attitude from complaining about, to rejoicing in, the suffering.

I also saw how I needed to be authentic. Not only could I share the medical miracle of change in my body but now I could also *share the change on the inside that the Lord had accomplished in me.* Until we live from His power on the inside, we are living in religion, no different from any other works-based worldview. But when we know it is God who changes our hearts by giving us His heart, born by His Spirit—we want to give ourselves to Him and let others know what He has done for us. We seek greater focus on Jesus and become thankful that His cross is central to our lives.

Like Jonah, who only spoke eight words from God and yet the city of Nineveh repented, my words to the father and his daughter were few but I know God can bring great change in their lives. I have assurance that the results are not up to me. My call is to obey God and share Christ.

"God is love" (1 John 4:8b ESV). "We love because He first loved us" (1 John 4:19 ESV). Will you let Jesus love you today? If you do not know Christ, will you repent and forsake your sin and enter into a covenant relationship and friendship with Jesus as Savior?

Jesus gave more than His life. He took sin, death, hell, the flesh, and the devil and overcame them all. Jesus said, "… take heart; I have overcome the world" (John 16:33b ESV). These experiences with the Lord brought me to want to live 2 Chronicles 7:14 and Revelation 12:11 together. I would not want to live any other way. This is a call of this book. This Gospel living is available to all believers.

Prayer

Lord, Thank You for giving Paul a second chance. Thank you for giving me a second chance physically and spiritually. Thank you for giving Jonah a second chance and saving Nineveh. Thank you that when Jonah obeyed you by speaking only eight words, You brought forth amazing results. Help us realize Your Word does not come back void but will accomplish Your purpose (Isaiah 55:11) and that obedience to You brings results. Help us to **be willing** to obey You, especially in living the great commission to go and share the Gospel with those You put in our paths. Help us realize what is at stake and share with confidence through Your Spirit. May we be determined to share You and Your Truths daily. Help us In Christ and His Gospel *bless all the nations.* Help us live knowing You, loving You, remembering You and telling about You through Your Story and our stories as You lead. May we **be willing** to receive and believe Your love for us, then express our love for You by our obedience and loyalty to You and our sharing of You with the world, In Jesus' Name, Amen.

Chapter Twenty-Five

Remembering Christ
Richard

"I (Jesus) made known to them your name (Heavenly Father), and I will continue to make it known, that the love with which you have loved me may be in them, and I in them." (John 17:26 ESV)

"For I received from the Lord what I also delivered to you, that the Lord Jesus on the night when he was betrayed took bread, and when he had given thanks, he broke it, and said, "This is my body, which is for you. Do this in remembrance of me." In the same way also he took the cup, after supper, saying, "This cup is the new covenant in my blood. Do this, as often as you drink it, in remembrance of me." For as often as you eat this bread and drink the cup, you proclaim the Lord's death until he comes."

(1 Corinthians 11:23-26 ESV).

One of the most intimidating functions for me to perform, yet one of the most rewarding at the same time, is to speak in front of a group of people and discuss our Lord and Savior Jesus Christ and all that He has done for me.

It is intimidating because I am speaking about the One who gave His life for me so I want to honor Him and properly recognize what He has done. It is rewarding because inevitably the Holy Spirit takes over while I am speaking, and I feel such confidence and joy. **I want so much for all who are present to experience the blessings that I have received from the Lord Jesus Christ.**

One of these functions for me is at our church. Our pastor asked me to provide a statement to the congregation to help each person prepare to partake of the elements of Holy Communion. The last time the Pastor asked me to provide the Communion preparation statement, I happened to be standing with two friends. When these friends heard what the

Pastor asked me to do, they both immediately brightened, saying that they had recently been at another Communion service and the gentleman providing the preparation statement used the story of Joseph in the Old Testament. They said that they were very impressed and blessed by the presentation because they had never noticed the connection between parts of Joseph's life and Holy Communion. I told them that I had not ever heard of that connection either and that I wished I had heard that presentation.

Unfortunately, before I could ask my friends to provide me with a summary of what had been said, we were interrupted, and I was left without any additional information. I decided I would try to determine the connection myself. I did a lot of praying and reflecting on Joseph's life.

One thing that becomes clear when studying the people and stories in the Old Testament is that many act as a pointer to, or forerunner of, Jesus Christ. We see circumstances and situations in the lives of the Old Testament figures that parallel the circumstances and situations in Christ's life. This is especially evident in the study of Joseph, as reflected in the following:

1. **Betrayal.** Joseph was betrayed by his brothers and sold into slavery. Certainly, the favoritism shown by Joseph's father, Jacob, as well as Joseph's pridefulness were factors in the betrayal. Joseph's brothers had learned to hate Joseph. The betrayal was still a painful and life changing event, which required Joseph to cling to his faith in Yahweh. Jesus was also betrayed by someone close to him, Judas Iscariot. Pride was also a factor in Jesus' betrayal, but it was not Jesus' pride, but rather the pride of Judas Iscariot and the ruling Pharisees and Sadducees in Israel. The fact that Judas could betray Jesus after spending the prior three years with Jesus during Jesus' earthly ministry, must have greatly grieved Jesus. Jesus had to cling to the Father's will and plan, as was clearly seen in the Garden at Gethsemane.
2. **Imprisonment.** Both Joseph and Jesus were imprisoned after being falsely accused of crimes. In both cases, though, Joseph and Jesus did not complain or become filled with self-pity. It seems that both men had such a close connection with God the Father which gave them a peace that passes all understanding even in the hard situations of life.
3. **Bread and Wine.** During the course of Joseph's imprisonment, he gained the trust and confidence of his jailers. When two high ranking individuals in Pharaoh's court were sent to prison by Pharaoh, Joseph was assigned the responsibility and duty to assist and attend to them until Pharaoh determined their guilt or innocence. The two high ranking individuals were the Chief Cup Bearer for Pharaoh and the Chief

Baker for Pharaoh. In these two men, we see the elements of Holy Communion—the bread and the wine. Joseph took advantage of "the bread and wine" that were available to him so that he might be remembered and set free. Jesus seeks to give us the bread and wine as a practice by which He would be remembered for what He has done for us, and so that we might commune with Him and be set free.

4. **Two Prisoners.** The Chief Cup Bearer and the Chief Baker were important men. On the same night during the time of their imprisonment, each of these high ranking individuals had a dream. They were puzzled by their dreams and wanted to find someone who could interpret the dreams for them. Joseph confidently told them that God was the interpreter of dreams, and that they should tell him their dreams so that God would properly interpret them. After hearing the two dreams and being led by the Holy Spirit, Joseph advised the Chief Cup Bearer that he would be restored to his position with Pharaoh in three days and that all would be well. Joseph advised the Chief Baker that in three days, Pharaoh would sentence the Chief Baker to death by hanging on a tree and that birds would eat his flesh. Similarly, Jesus had two fellow prisoners with whom He interacted. We read in the gospels how Jesus and the two thieves were sentenced to death by crucifixion. During the time of their crucifixion, Jesus interacted with the two thieves, who sought to understand who Jesus was and why He did not rescue himself. Ultimately, the one prisoner is restored to his position with the King of all Kings because he saw and accepted Jesus for who He is, while the other prisoner is crucified and birds eat his flesh; just like the Chief Cup Bearer and the Chief Baker.
5. **Remember.** After Joseph reveals the truth behind the dream of the Chief Cup Bearer and knows that the Chief Cup Bearer will be restored to good standing with Pharaoh, Joseph pleads with the Chief Cup Bearer to *remember him* to Pharaoh. Joseph knows that he has been unjustly imprisoned and is hopeful that if Pharaoh only knew the truth of his situation, Pharaoh would release him. Sadly and unfortunately, we read in the Old Testament that the Chief Cup Bearer *did not remember* Joseph until a number of years later. We can only imagine how the silence weighed on Joseph during those long years. He had been a faithful attendant to the Chief Cup Bearer during his imprisonment. He had been there to help the Chief Cup Bearer with the dream that clearly puzzled him and intrigued him. Joseph's interpretation should have been the encouragement that the Chief Cup Bearer needed to maintain his belief in justice, and to seek this for Joseph. All that Joseph did was worthy of being

remembered and should have caused the Chief Cup Bearer to remember and do what Joseph had asked.

When Jesus shared the bread and wine of the Last Supper, he, too, asked that we **remember Him.** He knew He was going to the cross to be the sacrifice to atone for our sins. His death would enable those who believe in Him, to be restored to and placed in good standing with God the Father. We will never be able to fully appreciate the **magnitude of what Christ has done for us,** but even with what we do know, **we should remember Him;** and, we will have the joy in eternity to show Him our appreciation.

Unlike the Chief Cup Bearer in failing to remember Joseph, **<u>will you remember Jesus and all that He has done?</u>** Joseph certainly was very helpful to the Chief Cup Bearer but **what Jesus has done and is doing, is infinitely more worthy of being remembered.** Further, ***by remembering Jesus and acknowledging Him as our Savior,*** *we continue to gain as we are led by the Holy Spirit and conformed to the likeness of our Savior.*

And ***he took bread, gave thanks and broke it, and gave it to them, saying, "This is my body given for you; <u>do this in remembrance of me.</u>"*** *In the same way, after the supper* ***he took the cup, saying, "This cup is the new covenant in my blood, which is poured out for you. (Luke 22:19,20 ESV)***

Partaking of the Communion elements is designed to cause us to remember Christ for He purchased our salvation- He paid our sin debts! We are called to remember His great sacrifice: the bread symbolizing Christ's body broken for us, and the wine symbolizing Christ's blood poured out for us for the forgiveness of our sins! These are things to remember and celebrate! The Communion ceremony is **designed to cause us <u>to remember</u>, to be thankful and <u>willing</u> <u>to</u> <u>share</u> <u>all</u> that <u>Christ</u> <u>has</u> <u>done</u> <u>for</u> <u>us</u>. *<u>Will you?</u>***

We are called to remember Christ's great sacrifice and death and its great significance in all four of the Gospels and in many places in the New Testament (Mt. 26:17–30; Mark 14:12-26; Lk. 22:7–39; John 6:53-58; 1 Corinthians 11:23-26: Acts 2:42-47 and 20:7; John 6:29-35,40,44,48-51;...)

Prayer

Heavenly Father, help us "remember Jesus" daily as we live and as we tell our stories. May the words we use to share Christ be in Your power to salvation. (Romans 1:16) May we not be ashamed of the Gospel. May the "saving of the lives of many" (Genesis 50:20) come about LORD. May we remember Jesus, in a special way by placing "the memory of

His Love at the Cross," over all the things we want to forget and really live forgiven! When we do this, Lord, help us give thanks to Jesus for His love and forgiveness, and cause His redemption to trump all the feelings that come with abuse and sin. May the word of our testimony be with the Revelation 12:11 confidence of Christ's overcoming by His blood. May we be convinced of Christ as the Lamb of God who takes away the sins of the world (John 1:29). Thank you, Jesus for coming to save us from our sin (Matthew 1:21). Help us celebrate, in **our remembrance of Christ,** through the breaking of the bread (Christ's body broken for us) and the drinking of the wine (Christ's blood shed for the forgiveness of our sin) the greatness of Christ and His forgiveness. May we often partake of communion and proclaim the Lord's death until He comes again, In Jesus' Name, Amen.

Important Prayers

(Listed for readers convenience with versions noted):

JESUS' PRAYERS in Matthew 6:8-13 (THE LORD'S PRAYER):

So do not be like them [praying as they do]; for your Father knows what you need before you ask Him. "Pray, then, in this way: 'Our Father, who is in heaven, Hallowed be Your name. Your kingdom come,Your will be done On earth as it is in heaven. 'Give us this day our daily bread.'And forgive us our [g]debts, as we have forgiven our debtors [letting go of both the wrong and the resentment]. 'And do not lead us into temptation, but deliver us from evil. For Yours is the kingdom and the power and the glory forever. Amen.' For if you forgive others their trespasses [their reckless and willful sins], your heavenly Father will also forgive you. 15 But if you do not forgive others [nurturing your hurt and anger with the result that it interferes with your relationship with God], then your Father will not forgive your trespasses (AMP).

JESUS' PRAYER IN JOHN 17:

Jesus Prays for the Father to Glorify Him

17 When Jesus had finished saying these things, he looked upward to heaven and said,
"Father, the time has come. Glorify your Son, so that your Son may glorify you— **2** just as
you have given him authority over all humanity, so that he may give eternal life to everyone
you have given him. **3** Now this is eternal life—that they know you, the only true God, and
Jesus Christ, whom you sent. **4** I glorified you on earth by completing the work you gave
me to do. **5** And now, Father, glorify me at your side with the glory I had with you before
the world was created.

Jesus Prays for the Disciples

6 "I have revealed your name to the men you gave me out of the world. They belonged to
you, and you gave them to me, and they have obeyed your word. **7** Now they understand
that everything you have given me comes from you, **8** because I have given them the words

you have given me. They accepted them and really understand that I came from you, and they believed that you sent me. **9** I am praying on behalf of them. I am not praying on behalf of the world, but on behalf of those you have given me, because they belong to you. **10** Everything I have belongs to you, and everything you have belongs to me, and I have been glorified by them. **11** I am no longer in the world, but they are in the world, and I am coming to you. Holy Father, keep them safe in your name that you have given me, so that they may be one just as we are one. **12** When I was with them I kept them safe and watched over them in your name that you have given me. Not one of them was lost except the one destined for destruction, so that the scripture could be fulfilled. **13** But now I am coming to you, and I am saying these things in the world, so they may experience my joy completed in themselves. **14** I have given them your word, and the world has hated them, because they do not belong to the world, just as I do not belong to the world. **15** I am not asking you to take them out of the world, but that you keep them safe from the evil one. **16** They do not belong to the world just as I do not belong to the world. **17** Set them apart in the truth; your word is truth. **18** Just as you sent me into the world, so I sent them into the world. **19** And I set myself apart on their behalf, so that they too may be truly set apart.

Jesus Prays for Believers Everywhere

20 "I am not praying only on their behalf, but also on behalf of those who believe in me through their testimony, **21** that they will all be one, just as you, Father, are in me and I am in you. I pray that they will be in us, so that the world will believe that you sent me. **22** The glory you gave to me I have given to them, that they may be one just as we are one— **23** I in them and you in me—that they may be completely one, so that the world will know that you sent me, and you have loved them just as you have loved me.

24 "Father, I want those you have given me to be with me where I am, so that they can see my glory that you gave me because you loved me before the creation of the world. **25** Righteous Father, even if the world does not know you, I know you, and these men know that you sent me. **26** I made known your name to them, and I will continue to make it known, so that the love you have loved me with may be in them, and I may be in them. (NET)

<u>THE PRAYERS OF PAUL IN THE EPISTLES: (ALL IN NET version except first verse)</u>

Philippians 3:8 Indeed, I count everything as loss because of the surpassing worth of knowing Christ Jesus my Lord. For his sake I have suffered the loss of all things and count them as rubbish, in order that I may gain Christ (ESV).

Romans 1:8-10 Paul's Desire to Visit Rome: First of all, I thank my God through Jesus Christ for all of you, because your faith is proclaimed throughout the whole world. For God, whom I serve in my spirit by preaching the gospel of his Son, is my witness that I continually remember you and I always ask in my prayers, if perhaps now at last I may succeed in visiting you according to the will of God (NET)

Romans 10:10: Brothers and sisters, my heart's desire and prayer to God on behalf of my fellow Israelites is for their salvation.

Romans 12:12 Rejoice in hope, endure in suffering, persist in prayer.

Romans 15:5-6 Now may the God of endurance and comfort give you unity with one another in accordance with Christ Jesus, so that together you may with one voice glorify the God and Father of our Lord Jesus Christ.

Romans 15:13 Now may the God of hope fill you with all joy and peace as you believe in him, so that you may abound in hope by the power of the Holy Spirit

Romans 15:30-33: Now I urge you, brothers and sisters, through our Lord Jesus Christ and through the love of the Spirit, to join fervently with me in prayer to God on my behalf. **31** Pray that I may be rescued from those who are disobedient in Judea and that my ministry in Jerusalem may be acceptable to the saints, so that by God's will I may come to you with joy and be refreshed in your company.Now may the God of peace be with all of you. Amen

1 Corinthians 14:9 It is the same for you. If you do not speak clearly with your tongue, how will anyone know what is being said? For you will be speaking into the air.

1 Corinthians 16:23 The grace of the Lord Jesus be with you.

2 Corinthians 1:3-7 Thanksgiving for God's Comfort: Blessed is the God and Father of our Lord Jesus Christ, the Father of mercies and God of all comfort, who comforts us in all our troubles so that we may be able to comfort those experiencing any trouble with the comfort with which we ourselves are comforted by God. For just as the sufferings of Christ overflow toward us, so also our comfort through Christ overflows to you. But if we are afflicted, it is

for your comfort and salvation; if we are comforted, it is for your comfort that you experience in your patient endurance of the same sufferings that we also suffer. And our hope for you is steadfast because we know that as you share in our sufferings, so also you will share in our comfort.

2 Corinthians 2:14-16 Apostolic Ministry: But thanks be to God who always leads us in triumphal procession in Christ and who makes known through us the fragrance that consists of the knowledge of him in every place. For we are a sweet aroma of Christ to God among those who are being saved and among those who are perishing— to the latter an odor from death to death, but to the former a fragrance from life to life. And who is adequate for these things?

2 Corinthians 9:12-15 because the service of this ministry is not only providing for the needs of the saints but is also overflowing with many thanks to God. Through the evidence of this service they will glorify God because of your obedience to your confession in the gospel of Christ and the generosity of your sharing with them and with everyone. And in their prayers on your behalf they long for you because of the extraordinary grace God has shown to you. Thanks be to God for his indescribable gift!

2 Corinthians 12:7-9 even because of the extraordinary character of the revelations. Therefore, so that I would not become arrogant, a thorn in the flesh was given to me, a messenger of Satan to trouble me—so that I would not become arrogant. I asked the Lord three times about this, that it would depart from me. But he said to me, "My grace is enough for you, for my power is made perfect in weakness." So then, I will boast most gladly about my weaknesses, so that the power of Christ may reside in me.

2 Corinthians 13:7-9 Now we pray to God that you may not do anything wrong, not so that we may appear to have passed the test, but so that you may do what is right even if we may appear to have failed the test. For we cannot do anything against the truth, but only for the sake of the truth. For we rejoice whenever we are weak, but you are strong. And we pray for this: that you may become fully qualified.

Galatians 6:18 The grace of our Lord Jesus Christ be with your spirit, brothers and sisters. Amen

Ephesians 1:3 Spiritual Blessings in Christ: Blessed is the God and Father of our Lord Jesus Christ, who has blessed us with every spiritual blessing in the heavenly realms in Christ.

Ephesians 1:15-23 Prayer for Wisdom and Revelation: For this reason, because I have heard of your faith in the Lord Jesus and your love for all the saints, I do not cease to give thanks for you when I remember you in my prayers. I pray that the God of our Lord Jesus Christ, the Father of glory, may give you spiritual wisdom and revelation in your growing knowledge of him, —since the eyes of your heart have been enlightened—so that you may know what is the hope of his calling, what is the wealth of his glorious inheritance in the saints, and what is the incomparable greatness of his power toward us who believe, as displayed in the exercise of his immense strength. This power he exercised in Christ when he raised him from the dead and seated him at his right hand in the heavenly realms far above every rule and authority and power and dominion and every name that is named, not only in this age but also in the one to come. And God *put all things under* Christ's *feet*, and he gave him to the church as head over all things. Now the church is his body, the fullness of him who fills all in all.

Ephesians 3:13-21 For this reason I ask you not to lose heart because of what I am suffering for you, which is your glory. Prayer for Strengthened Love: For this reason I kneel before the Father, from whom every family in heaven and on the earth is named. I pray that according to the wealth of his glory he may grant you to be strengthened with power through his Spirit in the inner person, that Christ may dwell in your hearts through faith, so that, because you have been rooted and grounded in love, you may be able to comprehend with all the saints what is the breadth and length and height and depth, and thus to know the love of Christ that surpasses knowledge, so that you may be filled up to all the fullness of God. Now to him who by the power that is working within us is able to do far beyond all that we ask or think, to him be the glory in the church and in Christ Jesus to all generations, forever and ever. Amen

Ephesians 6:19-20 Pray for me also, that I may be given the message when I begin to speak—that I may confidently make known the mystery of the gospel, for which I am an ambassador in chains. Pray that I may be able to speak boldly as I ought to speak.

Philippians 1:3-6 Prayer for the Church: I thank my God every time I remember you. I always pray with joy in my every prayer for all of you because of your participation in the gospel from the first day until now. For I am sure of this very thing, that the one who began a good work in you will perfect it until the day of Christ Jesus.

Philippians 1:9-11 And I pray this, that your love may abound even more and more in knowledge and every kind of insight so that you can decide what is best, and thus be sincere and blameless for the day of Christ, filled with the fruit of righteousness that comes through Jesus Christ to the glory and praise of God.

Philippians 4:6-7 Do not be anxious about anything. Instead, in every situation, through prayer and petition with thanksgiving, tell your requests to God. And the peace of God that surpasses all understanding will guard your hearts and minds in Christ Jesus.

Philippians 4:23 The grace of the Lord Jesus Christ be with your spirit.

Colossians 1:3-14 Paul's Thanksgiving and Prayer for the Church: We always give thanks to God, the Father of our Lord Jesus Christ, when we pray for you, since we heard about your faith in Christ Jesus and the love that you have for all the saints. Your faith and love have arisen from the hope laid up for you in heaven, which you have heard about in the message of truth, the gospel that has come to you. Just as in the entire world this gospel is bearing fruit and growing, so it has also been bearing fruit and growing among you from the first day you heard it and understood the grace of God in truth. You learned the gospel from Epaphras, our dear fellow slave—a faithful minister of Christ on our behalf— who also told us of your love in the Spirit. Paul's Prayer for the Growth of the Church: For this reason we also, from the day we heard about you, have not ceased praying for you and asking God to fill you with the knowledge of his will in all spiritual wisdom and understanding, so that you may live worthily of the Lord and please him in all respects—bearing fruit in every good deed, growing in the knowledge of God, being strengthened with all power according to his glorious might for the display of all patience and steadfastness, joyfully giving thanks to the Father who has qualified you to share in the saints' inheritance in the light. He delivered us from the power of darkness and transferred us to the kingdom of the Son he loves, in whom we have redemption, the forgiveness of sins.

Colossians 4:2-4 Exhortation to Pray for the Success of Paul's Mission: Be devoted to prayer, keeping alert in it with thanksgiving. At the same time pray for us too, that God may open a door for the message so that we may proclaim the mystery of Christ, for which I am in chains. Pray that I may make it known as I should.

1 Thessalonians 1:2-3 Thanksgiving for Response to the Gospel: We thank God always for all of you as we mention you constantly in our prayers, because we recall in the presence of our God and Father your work of faith and labor of love and endurance of hope in our Lord Jesus Christ.

1 Thessalonians 2:13-16 And so we too constantly thank God that when you received God's message that you heard from us, you accepted it not as a human message, but as it truly is, God's message, which is at work among you who believe. For you became imitators, brothers and sisters, of God's churches in Christ Jesus that are in Judea, because you too suffered the same things from your own countrymen as they in fact did from the Jews, who killed both the Lord Jesus and the prophets and persecuted us severely. They are displeasing to God and are opposed to all people, because they hinder us from speaking to the Gentiles so that they may be saved. Thus they constantly fill up their measure of sins, but wrath has come upon them completely.

1 Thessalonians 3:9-13 For how can we thank God enough for you, for all the joy we feel because of you before our God? We pray earnestly night and day to see you in person and make up what may be lacking in your faith. Now may God our Father himself and our Lord Jesus direct our way to you. And may the Lord cause you to increase and abound in love for one another and for all, just as we do for you, so that your hearts are strengthened in holiness to be blameless before our God and Father at the coming of our Lord Jesus with all his saints.

1 Thessalonians 5:23-24,28 Conclusion: Now may the God of peace himself make you completely holy and may your spirit and soul and body be kept entirely blameless at the coming of our Lord Jesus Christ. He who calls you is trustworthy, and he will in fact do this. The grace of our Lord Jesus Christ be with you.

2 Thessalonians 1:3,11-12 Thanksgiving: We ought to thank God always for you, brothers and sisters, and rightly so, because your faith flourishes more and more and the love of each

one of you all for one another is ever greater. And in this regard we pray for you always, that our God will make you worthy of his calling and fulfill by his power your every desire for goodness and every work of faith, that the name of our Lord Jesus may be glorified in you, and you in him, according to the grace of our God and the Lord Jesus Christ.

2 Thessalonians 2:16-17 Now may our Lord Jesus Christ himself and God our Father, who loved us and by grace gave us eternal comfort and good hope, encourage your hearts and strengthen you in every good thing you do or say.

2 Thessalonians 3:2-5 and that we may be delivered from perverse and evil people. For not all have faith. But the Lord is faithful, and he will strengthen you and protect you from the evil one. And we are confident about you in the Lord that you are both doing—and will do—what we are commanding. Now may the Lord direct your hearts toward the love of God and the endurance of Christ.

2 Thessalonians 3:16 Now may the Lord of peace himself give you peace at all times and in every way. The Lord be with you all.

1 Timothy 1:12 I am grateful to the one who has strengthened me, Christ Jesus our Lord, because he considered me faithful in putting me into ministry,

1 Timothy 2:1 Prayer for All People: First of all, then, I urge that requests, prayers, intercessions, and thanks be offered on behalf of all people,

2 Timothy 1:3-7 Thanksgiving and Charge to Timothy: I am thankful to God, whom I have served with a clear conscience as my ancestors did, when I remember you in my prayers as I do constantly night and day. As I remember your tears, I long to see you, so that I may be filled with joy. I recall your sincere faith that was alive first in your grandmother Lois and in your mother Eunice, and I am sure is in you. Because of this I remind you to rekindle God's gift that you possess through the laying on of my hands. For God did not give us a Spirit of fear but of power and love and self-control.

2 Timothy 1:16-18 May the Lord grant mercy to the family of Onesiphorus, because he often refreshed me and was not ashamed of my imprisonment. But when he arrived in Rome, he

eagerly searched for me and found me. May the Lord grant him to find mercy from the Lord on that day! And you know very well all the ways he served me in Ephesus.

2 Timothy 4:22 The Lord be with your spirit. Grace be with you.

Titus 3:15 Everyone with me greets you. Greet those who love us in the faith. Grace be with you all.

Philemon 4-7, 25 Thanks for Philemon's Love and Faith: I always thank my God as I remember you in my prayers, because I hear of your faith in the Lord Jesus and your love for all the saints. I pray that the faith you share with us may deepen your understanding of every blessing that belongs to you in Christ. I have had great joy and encouragement because of your love, for the hearts of the saints have been refreshed through you, brother. May the grace of the Lord Jesus Christ be with your spirit.

Appendix

INFORMATIONAL TEXTS ABOUT THE TOPIC OF SHARING CHRIST

If You Care, Will You Prepare?

Will You?

"SHARE CHRIST AS THE GREATEST TREASURE"

Deborah

The Purpose of This Book (Referring to The Bible, specifically The Gospel of John); (also a goal of this book):

[30] Now Jesus did many other signs in the presence of the disciples, which are not written in this book; [31] but these are ***written so that you may believe that Jesus is the Christ, the Son of God, and that by believing you may have life in his name. (John 20:30-31 ESV)***

"The kind of faith that saves a soul is one that transforms a life (James 2:26; 1 John 3:9-10) and rests fully on the grace of God."[42]

Therefore we ought to give the more earnest heed to the things which we have heard, lest at any time we should let them slip.For if the word spoken by angels was stedfast, and every transgression and disobedience received a just recompence of reward; How shall we escape, if we neglect so great salvation; which at the first began to be spoken by the Lord, and was confirmed unto us by them that heard him; God also bearing them witness, both with signs and wonders, and with divers miracles, and gifts of the Holy Ghost, according to his own will? For unto the angels hath he not put in subjection the world to come, whereof we speak (Hebrews 2:1-5 KJV).

If our soul is truly saved and our life has been transformed and rests fully on the grace of God, don't we have the power of the cross to solve the power of sin in this world? If so, why does God's power not show more in my life and others? I submit that, the Power of God to Salvation comes with not being ashamed of the Gospel and sharing Christ. (Romans 1:16)

For those readers who have not been born from above, we are told throughout the Bible especially in John 20:30-31 that what has been **written is for people so that they may believe that Jesus is the Christ, the Son of God, and that by believing they may have life in His Name.** In the process of coming to Christ we learn the truth of who God is and what He has done and His overall plan for His creation! Romans 10:17 says,"So then faith *comes* by hearing, and hearing by the word of God." If we have not believed we do not have eternal life!

The primary purpose of our witnessing to others and sharing with others is to join in the mission and power of God's Word to save the world. We are called to speak the Word of God so people can hear and hearing to bring them to faith by the Holy Spirit!

If we have believed will we care about the next person as God commissioned us in Matthew28:16-20?

Even if we care, there seems to be many reasons why sharing Christ is a struggle or is rare or absent in some believers lives. Could the main reason be a lack of remembering who Christ is and what Christ has really done for each of us on the cross?

Even when we remember, it can be difficult to know how to go about sharing and overcome unbelief, as I shared in Chapters 2 and 3. I have wrestled with the fact that on my own I can't make any difference and that's basically true. But if I give out God's message by His Spirit (John 15:1-5) God brings forth His fruit. His Word promises not to let His word come back void, Isaiah 55. Fear, lack of know-how, apathy, feeling like my faith is not working so why share it, and hurts caused by others, need to be overcome, so that we can move forward in faith and obedience to share.

When we recognize the remedy for sin and the real price of redemption, care and passion can result. A principle in life: when we care, we act, we speak. **Then, perhaps, we will join others in prayer and in unity to reach out to the lost with our greatest treasure Christ!**

If we don't care, why don't we care? Do we truly know Christ? If so, do we understand that the only reason we are secure in our born-again, born-of-the-Spirit state is because of Jesus? Only Jesus' work on the Cross and not our work, saved us. Do we know and appreciate and CARE about our great salvation? If yes, is Jesus our greatest treasure? Do we want others to know Him? If not why not?

You're blessed when you care. At the moment of being 'care-full,' you find yourselves cared for (Matthew 5:7 MSG)

Blessed are the merciful: for they shall obtain mercy (Matthew 5:7 KJV).

We must not let the cold water or cold blankets of unbelief in the world, the flesh, the devil and /or from other people put out the fire of the Holy Spirit. Sharing God's Word, sharing Christ, sharing His Gospel, matters.

We are commissioned (Matthew 28:16-20) by Jesus to be speakers, witnesses for Christ to live our faith. Most of us who have heard the gospel and received it, may be, (like I realized about myself), unprepared to share it. This appendix's purpose is to help us address preparedness. It is just a first step.

The LORD desires we become like Him by being loving, accepting, gracious, merciful, forgiving, and faithful always. The Lord desires for us to be willing to come to Christ (John 5:39-40), to know Christ, (Philippians 3:8,10-20) and to gain confidence in Christ so that the Gospel is our unshakable foundation. This is the rock foundation we are to live on as we "show and tell Christ". We want our lives to show others He is the way of true life (John 5:40) and salvation. (John 14:6; 17:3) We want others to see the change that Christ has made in us, our amazement at the magnitude of that change and the resulting joy which causes us to want to share our Lord and Savior.

This is what the first disciples lived. We see in the book of Acts how the resurrection of Christ and the coming of the Holy Spirit's power took them to a new level of living by the Holy Spirit that was clearly beyond their own flesh! The Holy Spirit in-dwelt them! Acts 1:8 states that the disciples of Christ would receive power when the Holy Spirit comes on them and they would be witnesses for Christ. Acts 1 and 2 retell the arrival of the promised Holy Spirit in fullness and miracles. The experience of Pentecost, **the indwelling of the Holy Spirit with power**, is to become **a present reality for believers** (Acts 2:29). The Lord promised to pour out His Spirit on all (Acts 2:17-21,Joel 2:28-32). We are to be powerful witnesses. Peter was. Full of the Holy Spirit, Peter tells of the wonder of the Bible, of Christ's plan of redemption: 3000 souls were saved. Some were those who had crucified Christ! How amazing is God's love and grace to offer forgiveness to us all, even those who were active in the crucifixion! This is Jesus, Savior of the world. Worthy is the Lamb, who takes away the sins of the world, Worthy of all honor, glory and praise, of all worship!

The book of Acts is important to us because we believers today are all witnesses of Christ's resurrection as truly born-again through the indwelling of the Holy Spirit. The transformation in us is to be evidence of Christ's resurrection. To know Christ is to care and want to share Him. If we don't care we must ask why? Are you truly saved? Do you know what Christ has done for you?

I hope that this book by the Holy Spirit workings, cause readers to truly realize the greatness of Christ, His salvation and thus care about others receiving Him! When we know Good News we share Good News. When we care we will prepare! This chapter contains a few important points to consider when sharing Jesus and our true Christian faith with others. Here are a few Scriptures and thoughts to hopefully better equip us to share the Gospel when we have an opportunity. First, think what you might say in order to lead someone to Christ? Maybe jot down the 3 most important points you might want to make. For me the three *initial* points are:

1. We all have a sin problem and Christ, as God's only Son, came to earth to bring the only solution. Jesus, out of perfect, complete and radical love for us died by crucifixion to pay the debt we owed and take our punishment so we could go to heaven. Scriptures to affirm this: 1 Corinthians 15:1-4: the death, burial, and resurrection of Jesus for the forgiveness of our sins; 1 John 1:9 and 2:1-2; Ephesians 1:7,13-14; Ephesians 2:1-7; Hebrews 9:22; Mark 10:45; Luke 5:31-32; John 3:16-17 **Jesus** paid (was) the **ransom for** the **repentant** to have **eternal life and not eternal punishment. (Matthew 25:46) (ABC: Accept, Believe, Confess)**
2. The Gospel is all the work of God and not of man. Jesus came to earth in humility and love to bring forgiveness. He died and rose for the forgiveness of our sins. He sent the Holy Spirit to indwell and guide those who have believed He is the Son of God and accepted Him as Lord and Savior. (Ephesians 2:8-9; John 1:13 and 14:17; 1 Corinthians 6:19-20; Titus 3:5; Colossians 1:27; Romans 8:15-17; 1 Corinthians 12:11; Romans 10:9-13 and many other verses)
3. Jesus said "Ye must be born again." John 3. We may know the commandments and live in a measure of obedience but we all fall short of God's glory. Thus, the only way to God the Father is through Jesus the Son. Once we accept and believe In Jesus and repent of our sins, we are indwelt by the Holy Spirit of promise. (Romans 3:23; 1 John 3:4; 1 John 5:17; a new heart and put a new spirit within you" Ezekiel 36:26; become new"; 2 Corinthians 5:17; 2 Peter 1:4; John 5:24).

Tim Keller has given a group of 3 words to characterize the real gospel and a group of the same three words in different order to show the "foolish Galatians" lifestyle. Paul told the

Galatians that they were living a cursed, false gospel of works, not of Christ. Which group of three words is the real gospel process and which one is a "false-trying to earn" one?

Believe
Saved
Obey
or
Believe
Obey
Saved

True salvation is received by grace and faith, while false salvation is based on trying to earn salvation. According to Ephesians 2:8-10, salvation is a gift of God not of works lest any should boast. After salvation, we are given Christ's righteousness and are empowered by the Holy Spirit to obey and do good works. (Romans 4, Ephesians 1-2)

On March 25, 2015, Author Timothy Keller tweeted:

"How Religion Works: If I obey, then God will love and accept me.

The Gospel: I'm loved and accepted; therefore, I wish to obey."

What is meant by "the different gospel" and "another Jesus" in the verses quoted in Chapters 1 and 2? How do we know if we know the real Jesus and the real gospel? Read the following Scriptures for more insight: Matthew 7:21-23; John 6:28-29; John 10:14; 1 John 3:23; Acts 15:1; Acts 15:5,10-11; Romans 5:8, 1 Corinthians 2:16 & 8:3; 15:1-4; Ephesians 2:8-10 and 3:17. A helpful article by David Wilkerson can be found at https://worldchallenge.org/newsletter/1991/another-jesus-another-spirit-another-gospel.

4. Tell what Jesus has done for you. Share what He leads you to share. Testify about Jesus. Tell of His coming, dying, rising for the forgiveness of your sins. Tell of His love, forgiveness, mercy and grace. We are witnesses and representatives of Christ. Everywhere you go, whether speaking or not, your life is a testimony. Make your life count for eternity by letting the Holy Spirit lead you. Be courageous. At your most difficult times, your testimony may be at its most powerful. Be quick to repent and apply the Gospel to yourself. Guard your heart from legalism or self-works but to live by His Grace. Be sowers of His Word, His Seed will prosper! The more we yield to the Holy Spirit the more harvest God produces.

5. Find joy in your relationship with Jesus. Until Jesus is our greatest treasure we will not treat Him as such or share Him as the Treasure He is! Pray for Him to be Your greatest treasure. Make your most important moments of each day spending time with Him in His Word and in worship and in prayer. Realize that worship fuels your life with His Presence. Worship is a great gift and the truth that God inhabits our praises (Psalm 22:3) is a promise and a motivation! The LORD's Presence can manifest in true worship! Cultivate your relationship with Jesus as the most important relationship and priority in your life. Love God with all you are. "Do not let your lips hug him but let your heart be far from Him." Give Him your heart and praise and love Him with your thoughts, words and actions and you will have the greatest life. May Christ be our greatest treasure and may we share Him passionately and powerfully!

Above is basic information on the main topic of

"Sharing CHRIST As Our Greatest Treasure"

It is not meant to be a complete guide. We pray you will make your own preparations to "Remember and Share Christ" as a main priority in your lives.

References and Resources:

BOOKS:

Absolutely Sober A History, Principle and Practice of the Destruction of Self-Centeredness, by George McLauchlin

Shadow of the Almighty The Life and Testament of Jim Elliot (Lives of Faith)by Elisabeth Elliot, Harper Collins

Wounded by God's People : Discovering How God's Love Heals Our Hearts by Anne Graham Lotz, Zondervan

Just Hold On by Denise Haas, Xulon Press

If I Had Two Lives The Extraordinary Life and Faith of Costa Macris by Dan Vorm, Clovercroft Publishing

The Mended Heart God's Healing for Your Broken Places by Suzanne Eller

Hidden Joy In A Dark Corner by Wendy Blight 2009 (2019 Bible Study of Proverbs 31 Ministries)

Love Dare by Stephen Kendrick and Alex Kendrick, B & H Publishing Group, 2008

Hind Feet in High Places by Hannah Hurnard

Mountains of Spices by Hannah Hurnard, Tyndale House Publishers

The Quest, Study Journal: An Excursion Toward Intimacy with God by Beth Moore, Lifeway

The Secret Thoughts of an Unlikely Convert : An English Professor's Journey into Christian Faith, by Rosaria Champagne Butterfield, Crown and Covenant Publications.

Jesus > Religion: Why He Is So Much Better Than Trying Harder, Doing More, and Being Good Enough by Jefferson Bethke, Thomas Nelson Publishers.

Learning to Speak God from Scratch Why Sacred Words Are Vanishing and How We Can Revive Them, by Jonathan Merritt, Convergent Books

Undaunted: One Man's Real-Life Journey from Unspeakable Memories to Unbelievable Grace, by Josh D. McDowell and Cristobal Krusen, Tyndale Momentum.

Undaunted Student Edition: Daring to Do What God Calls You to Do, by Christine Caine and Max Lucado, Zondervan.

The Harbinger, by Jonathan Cahn, Frontline, Charisma House Book Group, 2011.....

My Genes Made Me Do It! Homosexuality and the Scientific Evidence by NE and BK Whitehead

Sexuality in the New Testament by William Loader

Straight and Narrow? Compassion and Clarity in the Homosexuality Debate by Thomas Schmidt

FILMS:

Audacity, Film, directed by Ray Comfort, 2015, A Living Waters Production Available for free www. audacitymovie.com or https://www.youtube.com/watch?v=tbPu2rtmDbY

https://www.massresistance.org/docs/gen3/17d/MR-TX-Teens4Truth-Conf-101817/presentations.html (Mass Resistance, Teens4Truth Conference in November 2017 in Ft Worth, Texas.) For those interested in learning more this is the link to the conference and video presentations.

ARTICLES:

Article titled: When Abortion Suddenly Stopped Making Sense by Frederica Mathewes-Green January 22, 2016, National Review

How Wide the Divide: Sexuality at the Forefront, Culture at the Crossroads by Ravi Zacharias, Found at https://www.rzim.org/read/rzim-global/how-wide-the-divide-sexuality-at-the-forefront-culture-at-the-crossroads

"How much does an abortion cost? Well, from $0 to $3,275" by Theresa Fisher June 19, 2014 https://clearhealthcosts.com/blog/2014/06/much-abortion-cost-draft-theresas/

ncbi.nlm.nil.gov "Why Do Women Have Abortions" guttmacher.org "Reasons US Women Have Abortions: Quantitative and Qualitative Perspectives")

https://www.psychologytoday.com/us/blog/hide-and-seek/201509/when-homosexuality-stopped-being-mental-disorder and https://www.theguardian.com/society/2007/jun/24/communities.gayrights

http://www.allgirlsallowed.org/forced-abortion-statistics#_edn12

https://www.frc.org/twochildpolicy

https://www.abortionfacts.com/reardon/women-at-risk-of-post-abortion-trauma

https://www.heartbeatinternational.org/forced-abortions-in-america

(Although the pro-choice.org gives dramatically opposing statistics. https://5aa1b2xfmfh2e2mk03kk8rsx-wpengine.netdna-ssl.com/wp-content/uploads/women_who_have_abortions.pdf) There statistic revolves around the most important reason given for abortion only to give the 1% statistic.

https://www.usatoday.com/story/opinion/2013/06/17/gary-bauer-and-daniel-allott-on-forced-abortions/2432769/

RECOMMENDED WEBSITES:

https://www.gotquestions.org/who-will-go-to-heaven.html

https://www.rainn.org/articles/tips-talking-survivors-sexual-assault

Post-Abortive Help from American Victims of Abortion Website https://www.nrlc.org/outreach/ava/

Partial List of Abortion Related Information Web Sites

- Association for Interdisciplinary Research in Values and Social Change (post-abortion syndrome, PAS research)
- After Abortion (broad source of resources)
- Project Rachel (links to Project Rachel and Rachel's Vineyard Retreats, etc.)
- Bethesda The House of Mercy (excellent support resource)
- Fatherhood Forever Foundation (general information and help for men)
- Reclaiming Fatherhood (more services for men)
- ProLifeInfo.org (general info)
- Option Line (support and assistance for pregnant women)
- Silent No More (opportunities to share public testimonies)
- Her Choice (real audio clips of past testimonies from women and men)
- Ramah International (lots of PAS info and help)
- ________________________________
- Other Post-Abortive Help
- CARENET
- Passages of Hope
- New Life Solutions

****

Help for SSA and LGBTQ Lifestyle Redemption/Recovery:

Hope for Wholeness Network https://hopeforwholeness.org/new-hearts-outreach/

Endnotes

1 My father died of mesothelioma, a terrible lung cancer that is from asbestos exposure. His death was difficult. My mom, a smoker, had COPD (Chronic Obstructive Pulmonary Disease) and at times, had a severely difficult time breathing with coughs and lungs that sounded somewhat familiar to what I was hearing with the coughing man at the clinic. My mom succumbed to pneumonia her last days that caused heart a heart attack and ultimately cardiac arrest. As a nurse having watched many patients suffer prior to death, I have questioned if it would be easier to die a quick death than lingering, suffering, or be afflicted or in agony for a long time or unknown time. Suffering long term is brutal. Death can seem a reprieve or relief.

2 Tim Keller tweet, November 2018

3 Francis Frangipane "One Man" Article on Francis Frangipane Ministries June 7,2019 (http://www.ujtomlo.injesus.com/message-archives/christian-living/frangipane/one-man-5)

4 I want to be clear: The man denied any possibility of the money being earmarked for abortion, but I felt the woman's silence and seeming fear, the entirety of our conversation and the intensity of the encounter pointed to this real possibility. My husband and I lived in this type of denial for years. It was hard for us to admit our wrong intentions and for us, the deadly results. I understand how difficult it is. I have no proof this is what that couple intended. I have tried to be as factual as possible to share my experience and perceptions.

5 Dwight L. Moody Was Converted by Diane Severance, Ph.D. and Dan Graves, MSL (https://www.christianity.com/church/church-history/timeline/1801-1900/dwight-l-moody-was-converted-11630499.html

6 Disclaimer: My experiences at Firehouse were not planned and not in any way associated with Firehouse Subs as a restaurant. I simply happened to frequent the eatery and had extra-ordinary encounters there that had nothing to do with the actual restaurant itself. Firehouse Subs (Firehouse of America, LLC) is a U.S.-based, fast casual restaurant chain founded in 1994 in Jacksonville, Florida by former firefighter brothers Robin and Chris Sorensen. At Firehouse Subs, subs are only part of our story. A portion of your purchase in 2018 at all US Firehouse Subs locations goes to the Firehouse Subs Public Safety Foundation, to be used to provide lifesaving equipment to first responders. Since the Foundation started, it has granted over $37.7 million to provide equipment, training, and support to hometown heroes. All because at Firehouse Subs we believe that making great subs is not enough; you have to do good, too. Learn More at FirehouseSubsFoundation.org Information found at: https://www.firehousesubs.com/public-safety-foundation/ "Firehouse Subs is dedicated to firefighters and founded by firemen."

7 5 Ways Abortion Negatively Impacts Men by Warren Williams Posted by Care Net on January 6, 2016 - https://www.care-net.org/churches-blog/5-ways-abortion-negatively-impacts-men

8 https://www.ajog.org/article/S0002-9378(10)01176-2/fulltext Adverse childhood experiences and repeat induced abortion (American Journal of Obstretrics and Gyenocology Maria E. Bleil, PhDa

9 https://www.nrlc.org/outreach/ava/ (Abortion Information and statistics, National Right To Life, Since 1968)

10 https://www.nrlc.org/abortion/ (Abortion Information and statistics, National Right To Life, Since 1968)

11 US Abortion Attitudes Remain Closely Divided by Jeffrey M. Jones on June 11, 2018 at Gallup News https://news.gallup.com/poll/235445/abortion-attitudes-remain-closely-divided.aspx

12 Jonathan Cahn, The Harbinger: The Ancient Mystery that Holds the Secret of America's Future, Frontline Publisher.

13 https://www.christianpost.com/news/70-of-women-who-get-abortions-identify-as-christians-survey-finds.html 70% of Women Who Get Abortions Identify as Christians, Survey Finds by Samuel Smith, Christian Post, November 25, 2015

14 Why Are Evangelical Women at Planned Parenthood? What a recent Marie Claire report gets wrong—and right—about evangelicals and abortion. JULIE ROYS https://www.christianitytoday.com/women/2017/june/why-are-evangelical-women-planned-parenthood.html

15 "I can't deny the article's basic assertion that evangelicals are using Planned Parenthood, but I strongly deny the article's conclusion that Evangelicals need Planned Parenthood.""Why Are Evangelical Women at Planned Parenthood?" "What a recent Marie Claire Report gets wrong -and-right-about evangelicals and abortion" by Julie Roys in article in ChristianityToday.comhttps://www.christianitytoday.com/women/2017/june/why-are-evangelical-women-planned-parenthood.html

16 As quoted in the Washington Post, https://www.washingtonpost.com/news/early-lead/wp/2017/06/06/a-decision-that-broke-me-american-track-star-had-abortion-just-before-olympics/?utm_term=.c91d90a46205

17 from the article titled: "How Much Does An Abortion Cost? Well from $0 to $3,275" by Theresa Fisher June 19, 2014; https://clearhealthcosts.com/blog/2014/06/much-abortion-cost-draft-theresas/

18 Fatherhood Lost How Abortion Affects Men June 9, 2017 (This piece was originally published on Breakpoint and was written by Eric Metaxas.) Article @ https://savethestorks.com/2017/06/fatherhood-lost-abortion-aingtonffects-men/

19 numberofabortions.com Number of Abortions - Abortion Counters; Each real-time abortion counter is based on the most current statistics* for the number of abortions in the US & the number of abortions Worldwide. (US Abortion clock.org)

20 https://www.abortionfacts.com/reardon/women-at-risk-of-post-abortion-trauma

21 https://savethestorks.com/2017/06/fatherhood-lost-abortion-affects-men/ "Jesus made the option of a new identity for all people in His redemptive work on the Cross. He was in the world reconciling us to God." https://www.care-net.org/churches-blog/5-ways-abortion-negatively-impacts-men

22 https://www.thegospelcoalition.org/blogs/justin-taylor/the-remorse-of-abortion-and-the-healing-of-the-gospel-a-conversation-with-lecrae-john-piper-and-john-ensor/

23 Interview: Lecrae and John Piper and John Ensor (can see video or get transcript) https://www.thegospelcoalition.org/blogs/justin-taylor/the-remorse-of-abortion-and-the-healing-of-the-gospel-a-conversation-with-lecrae-john-piper-and-john-ensor/

24 Prayer based on interview of John Piper in audio Transcript (Episode 1067) "I Had an Abortion" July 14, 2017 found at DesiringGod.org

25 My Genes Made Me Do It Page 218-219 (Can sexual orientation change?) "Most teenagers will change from SSA. In fact, in the 16 to 17 year age group, 98% will move from homosexuality and bisexuality towards heterosexuality, perhaps experiencing some or exclusive opposite sex attraction for the first time.

Most teenagers thinking they are gay/lesbian/bi and will be for the rest of their life, will in fact probably be different the following year. It is therefore totally irresponsible, and flatly contradicted by the facts, to counsel affirmation of same-sex feelings in an adolescent on the grounds that the feelings are intrinsic, unchangeable, and the individual is therefore homosexual."

26 24/7 help at Call 800.656.HOPE (4673) Website full of helpful & supportive information https://www.rainn.org/articles/tips-talking-survivors-sexual-assault; Hope for Wholeness Network, https://hopeforwholeness.org.

27 See Endnote #6

28 http://www.nclrights.org/sexual-assault-in-the-lgbt-community/April 30, 2014 (Website for National Center for Lesbian Rights) Sexual Assault in the LGBT Community By Lauren Paulk, NCLR Reproductive Justice Fellow "…CDC **statistics that show** the sexual assault rate for LGBT individuals is comparable or higher than the sexual assault rate for heterosexual individuals. **Approximately 1 in 8 lesbian women and nearly half of bisexual women experience rape in their lifetime, and statistics likely increase when a broader definition of sexual assault is used. Nearly half of bisexual men and four in ten gay men have experienced sexual violence other than rape in their lifetime,** and though statistics regarding rape vary, it is likely that the rate is higher or comparable to heterosexual men. As with most hate-based violence, transgender individuals are the most likely to be affected in the LGBT community. A **staggering 64% of transgender people have experienced sexual assault in their lifetime.**

29 In U.S., Estimate of LGBT Population Rises to 4.5% (May 22, 2018) By Frank Newport https://news.gallup.com/poll/234863/estimate-lgbt-population-rises.aspx Rise in LGBT identification mostly among millennials *LGBT identification is lower among older generations *5.1% of women identify as LGBT, compared with 3.9% of men (There are other articles that show there are not as many gay people as many think. I encourage us to do the research.)

30 Look for Angela Adkin's book "Twice Broken" that should be coming out late 2019.

31 https://lindaseiler.com/

32 See Endnote #6

33 http://www.isna.org/faq/transgender One selection from this website that was most enlightening to me was as follows: "Many people confuse transgender and transsexual people with people with intersex conditions because they see two groups of people who would like to choose their own gender identity and sometimes those choices require hormonal treatments and/or surgery. These are similarities. It's also true, albeit rare, that some people who have intersex conditions also decide to change genders at some point in their life, so some people with intersex conditions might also identify themselves as transgender or transsexual. In spite of these similarities, these two groups should not be and cannot be thought of as one. The truth is that the vast majority of people with intersex conditions identify as male or female rather than transgender or transsexual." (my emphasis)

34 See Endnote #6

35 https://nyti.ms/2XjRMIA How Should Christians Have Sex? Purity culture was harmful and dangerous. But its collapse has left a void for those of us looking for guidance in our intimate lives. By Katelyn Beaty, June 15, 2019. Surely, we do not want to repeat failures in our attempts to teach and impact our youth. Perhaps a focus on Christ and relationship with Him and understanding the gift Christ is and the sacrifice of love on the cross will bring people to live at His feet and receive His power over our temptations. He helps us love as He loved us. It is sacrificial at times especially in our sexuality to obey His Word over living as the culture dictates.

36 A commentary for Acts 15 helped me sort out the above article in the NY Times with the meanings in the Word of God. (bolded for emphasis): "Peter went right to the heart of the question. In this whole

dispute the deepest of principles was involved. Can a man earn the favour of God? Or must he admit his own helplessness and be ready in humble faith to accept what the grace of God gives? In effect, the Jewish party said, "Religion means earning God's favour by keeping the Law." Peter said, "Religion consists in casting ourselves on the grace of God." Here is implicit the difference between a religion of works and a religion of grace. Peace will never come to a man until he realizes that he can never put God in his debt; and that all he can do is take what God in his grace gives. The paradox of Christianity is that the way to victory is through surrender; and the way to power is through admitting one's own helplessness…(https://www.studylight.org/commentaries/dsb/acts-15.html

37 "Hope for the family the gospel, hope, and the world" by Dr Timothy Keller, https://www.youtube.com/watch?v=R7htR6ovxDg

38 See Endnote #6

39 "Although this is the earliest chronological event of all I have written in this book, I share it last …. I added this: mainly for two main reasons: 1. Without what the Lord did throughout that time frame, I do not think I would have finished writing my first book. 2. God's second chances were vital to my life, health. call, freedom and future. Without the changes and how they affected my actions I would not be living as I am today. I hope to encourage the reader that, like Paul and Jonah, God sometimes does give second chances and they matter or can be pivotal in our lives and others.

40 Nicky Gumble, Day 163 of the APP, "YOU VERSION", Devotional titled ONE YEAR BIBLE 2019 BY NICKY GUMBLE

41 Jesus Commands Us to Tell Others, found at https://www.allaboutjesuschrist.org/jesus-commands-us-to-tell-others-faq.htm

42 https://www.gotquestions.org/who-will-go-to-heaven.html

CPSIA information can be obtained
at www.ICGtesting.com
Printed in the USA
JSHW020231160722
28170JS00002B/16

9 781545 672983